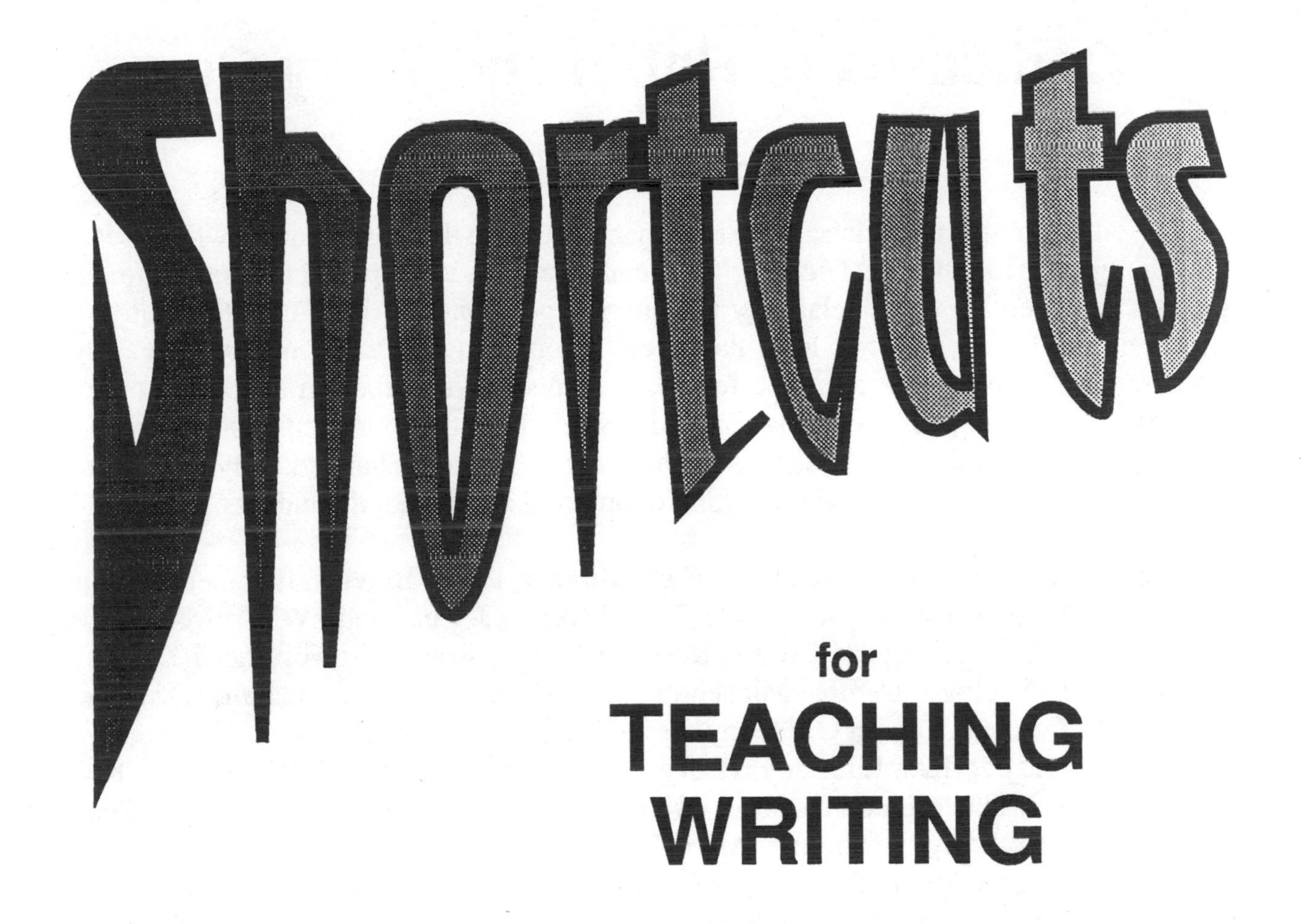

Shortcuts for TEACHING WRITING

by Flora Joy
Illustrated by Pat Harroll

Cover by Janet Skiles

ISBN No. 0-86653-590-X

Printing No. 98

Good Apple, Inc.
299 Jefferson Road
P.O. Box 480
Parsippany, NJ 07054-0480

Simon & Schuster Supplementary Education Group

Dedicated to Robin and Terry Cox

The author of this text wishes to extend many thanks to those individuals who posed for the photographs to illustrate ***The Neighborhood News.*** (A very special thanks is offered to those who posed for some relatively unflattering positions.) All of the stories in these rewritten articles are **true;** at least they were reported in *reputable newspapers* as **real events.** The purpose was to entice today's students to write about a situation or event. Securing photographs of the **actual** individuals to whom these happenings occurred was impossible. In most cases the names of the individuals were changed. My apologies to anyone who is embarrassed by a reporting of any of these included incidents.

Photo credits in alphabetical order: Carol Birkner, Penny Blevins, Elizabeth Bodkins, Barbara Burleson, Rick Burleson, Joyce Casteel, Teresa J. Cox, Betty W. Crowe, Carey C. Crowe, Irene Crowe, Kendra Crowe, Rebekka Crowe, Roger Crowe, Sherri Davidson, Shelly Dawes, Shelby J. Denton, Michelle Dotson, Tenna Drain, Regina Fair, Lisa Fedele, Marcella M. Fennell, Jennifer Gill, Tonya Grindstaff, Penny Hawkins, Iva D. Haynes, Lydia P. Hilliard, Andy Jeffers, Edna Joy, Henry F. Joy II, Henry F. Joy III, Candace L. Kiser, Lou K. Kiser, Michele Laurain, Susan Lyon, Amy Martin, Robert T. Martindale, Cecilia Reneé McClure, Tonya McInturff, Mary Margaret Miller, Janice Oaks, Janelle Patton, Beverly Pendergast, Sherry Penley, Joni P. Rees, Mary J. Roberts, Michelle Roberts, Cassie Sebastian, Tim Shelton, David L. Smith, Karen E. Smith, Robert Street, Chad Truman, Kimberly M. Vaughn, Pamela Vaughn, David A. White, and Carrie Williams.

Chief Photographer: Robin Cox.

Credits for "Mouth Traps" contributions: Mary Nelson, Kristy Meyers, Michelle Moorhouse, and Susan Hall.

TABLE OF CONTENTS

INTRODUCTION

WRITING ACTIVITIES

(A POSTER FOR WRITING CENTERS)

THE

CENTER

SHORTCUTS FOR TEACHING WRITING

AN INTRODUCTION

As an adult reader of this book, imagine you are being asked to complete the following assignment: *Write a five-page theme which addresses the political, economic, psychological, and social implications of a gradual increase in the local sales tax by one tenth of one percent.* Maybe you would be excited with such a writing challenge. Most of us would not.

A parallel may be drawn with younger writers. Although the above topic would be differently worded, the dread of completing a "writing assignment" may be the same.

Many education environments have evolved into academic pencil-and-paper tasks which require only multiple-choice or true-false responses. These are systems in which the learners **actually write** fewer and fewer complete thought units or longer passages. Some are systems in which learners very seldom ever write a complete sentence.

Where can blame be placed for such a scarcity of writing experiences? Classroom teachers certainly have little time to devote to the daily reading and scoring of long writing assignments. Most curricula are crammed with an abundance of "needed periphery." The result is that many of today's students may ultimately look forward to a lifetime of poor and ineffective written communication skills!

Most teachers cannot find the classroom time to have **each** student write a lengthy selection daily. Nor would most have the time to evaluate such writing properly. Although a "shortcut" to the problem might not be the best solution, the learning and using of **some** "shortcuts" for classroom organizational procedures may result in a far better alternative than **avoiding** the challenge of teaching writing altogether.

Thus a book entitled **Shortcuts for Teaching Writing** was prepared. The techniques offered in this text have been tested, revised, and retested with thousands of young writers. The users of this material should feel free to adapt any of the suggestions to fit the needs of the learners involved.

The first section begins with an explanation of a five-step writing plan, a description of a plan for correcting students' writing "mistakes," information on writing models, and suggestions for evaluation of students' writing performances. This section is followed by a variety of actual writing activities, most of which are ready to use. Others require a small amount of time in their preparation for classroom writing experiences. All are designed for busy teachers and for reluctant writers!

An important suggestion for all to remember is that the writing experience should always be a **positive one!**

Happy writing!

THE FIVE-STEP WRITING PLAN

Good writers do not generally *begin* by producing a best-selling novel! The writing task should be presented and developed in simple, logical and easily understood steps. The following five-step plan outlines such a procedure:

Step 1: THE WORD

Step 2: THE PHRASE

Step 3: THE SENTENCE

Step 4: THE PARAGRAPH

Step 5: THE STORY, Theme, Essay (or longer selection)

Please do not dismiss the above hierarchy as being too simple to use in teaching writing skills. Why make things more complicated than is necessary?

The rationale behind this five-step writing plan is as follows: It is difficult for students to write **stories, themes, essays, or longer selections** if they have not mastered the ability to write good paragraphs. They cannot construct well-worded **paragraphs** if they cannot write meaningful sentences. They are less able to create well-worded **sentences** if they have not experienced the writing of different types of **phrases.** They cannot write good phrases if they are unable to identify and select appropriate **words.**

Competence in writing at each of these levels is not an inborn ability for most learners. Instruction and practice are essential for building and reinforcing these skills. No matter the age or grade level of the learner, these steps should be approached in the above hierarchical manner. Periodic review and much practice in each of the levels is very beneficial to becoming a polished writer.

In the development of each step in this plan, learners should gain experiences both as individual and group writers. They should have writing conferences with the instructor, with classmates, and with volunteer school staff.

The exercises and activities in this text are designed to demonstrate how these groupings may occur and how the specific writing skills can be developed at each step in the above hierarchy. Any of these exercises may be used as an **oral activity** instead of an on-paper writing assignment whenever desired. These oral discussions may greatly expand the listeners' ideas and organizational patterns for later writing experiences.

Frequent use of the chalkboard during these discussions may aid the building of such skills. For example, at the phrase level (Step 2), the learners may be asked to write two descriptors of their best friend. If a list of possibilities appears in view (on the chalkboard), then the writers may have a wider variety of choices to make this phrase more meaningful by being able to select from words they already know and additionally seeing selected choices of others.

WRITING MODELS

An older method of teaching the writing of longer passages was to instruct learners to *make an outline, then fill it in with words*. The fallacy with this approach was that young writers were relatively ignorant of **how** to establish such an appropriate outline for a corresponding writing task. The outline method has gradually been replaced with the use of writing models. The latter has been more effective in helping students prepare a better and more polished writing product than the former method of outlining.

What is a writing model? A writing model serves as the guide for the major thoughts to be covered in the final written product. It is the writer's **plan of action.** Without it, the manuscript may be haphazard, incohesive, and illogical. The needed model can be compared to the blueprint for a house. Should the carpenters, plumbers, and electricians each proceed without such a guide, the final dwelling might be an impossible structure. The model can be as simple as a list of paragraph topics, preceded by an introduction and followed by a conclusion. Or it can resemble a table of contents of a text. The purpose of a writer establishing a writing model before completing **any** longer writing assignment is parallel to that of the instructor who prepares a lesson plan before teaching a class. ***It must be done for effective writing to result.*** Ultimately it is an essential time-saver in the writing process.

What is the procedure for using writing models? The procedure for using writing models varies with the age and skill of the writers. For younger writers, the model may start with relatively short passages, such as a three or four-paragraph narrative. This model can follow the "Lead in, Explain it, Wrap it up" style. The following is an example.

Title: My Funniest Relative
Model: **Lead in:** Identify the selected relative in one or more complete sentences.

Explain it: Give one or more specific examples of why this relative is funny. Each separate example should be in a different paragraph.

Wrap it up: Conclude the story with a final sentence about the humor or good nature of this relative.

My Funniest Relative
by Susie

In my family are many funny people. Aunt Emma always laughs when she tells a joke, and Cousin Mary giggles and grins quite often. Uncle George, however, wins the prize for being the funniest of all. He has played many pranks on his relatives and friends.

One day he dressed up like a clown and visited our class at school. He gave all of my classmates a lollipop and a balloon. He told corny jokes which made everyone roll on the floor. My friends at school asked him to come back many times.

Another funny time with Uncle George was when he tried to eat my sister's cooking. He grabbed his throat each time he took a bite, but he always winked at her when he did. Before the meal was over, my sister poured water on him. I thought he would get mad, but we all wound up laughing.

Uncle George always made people laugh. But when he died last month, I didn't feel much like laughing. I felt better, though, when the preacher said, "I know that Uncle George wants us all to keep a smile on our face." His memories will keep me smiling.

Other similar styles of writing models may follow these patterns:

- *Introduction*
- *Explanation*
- *Conclusion*

Or:

- *Topic (or Lead) Paragraph*
- *Supporting Paragraph(s)*
- *Summary Paragraph*

Writing models can proceed to longer and more detailed passages. It is not always enough, however, to provide students with a model. Frequently the **information** which will be used in the writing passage will need to be provided. For example, if a group of students were asked to write a factual essay entitled "The Koala," many of the responses might read as follows: *The koala is a furry little bear that lives in Australia.* This could be all they **know** about the koala. (In fact, it may reflect what they **don't** know, because a koala is not a bear at all.) Such a writing task should be preceded with a multitude of appealing examples (pictures, books, encyclopedia articles, etc.) and **much discussion.** A writing model could then be provided for the learners to follow. Such a model might be as follows:

The Koala

- *Introduction*
- *Appearance*
- *Classification in the Animal Kingdom*
- *Birth and Early Dependency*
- *Daily Routine*
- *Diet*
- *Social Aspects*
- *Survival*
- *Final Thought*

The following page provides one sample essay which followed the above model.

Many of the activities in the remainder of this book provide suggested models for learners to follow or at least consider in the writing of their material.

The thought to remember with modeling is that **the writing must be <u>planned</u> before the product is effective.**

Sample Writing Model

The Koala

The koala is an animal which has several habits and practices quite different from other living creatures. Most people have heard of the animal, but few know many facts about how it lives.

*The koala is an Australian mammal that **looks** like a tree-climbing teddy bear, though it is not related to any kind of bear. It has soft, thick fur, a large hairless nose, round ears, and no tail. The fur on its back is gray or brown, but it is white on the belly. It has sharp, curved claws, long toes, and a strong grip. The average koala is about 25-30 inches (63.5-76.2 cm) long and weighs from 15 to 30 pounds (6.75 to 13.5 kg).*

*Koalas are called **marsupials.** A marsupial is a mammal that gives birth to its young in an incomplete state of development. The young koala then completes the remainder of its early growth in the mother's pouch. A well-known marsupial is the kangaroo.*

Female koalas give birth to tiny, poorly developed offspring. The newborn koala is about as thick as a pencil and no more than an inch long. There is rarely more than one born at a time. Without help, this newborn crawls into its mother's pouch which is upside down. It does not fall out because it attaches itself firmly to the mother and cannot be removed without much force. It spends six months developing in this pouch, then it spends the next six months riding on the mother's back. Compared with other wild animals, the young koala remains dependent for a long period of time. It is still helpless when it is a year old. It is almost fully grown before it can take care of itself. In four years it reaches full growth and may live for as long as 20 years.

The daily routine of koalas might be considered very boring to us. Since they are active mainly at night, they sleep most of the day in the forks of eucalyptus trees. They spend a large part of their lives just clinging to trees, and they will come down out of the tree only to move to another tree. They are very adept at moving through the branches, but they are very awkward on the ground. For this reason they rarely leave their home in the trees.

The diet of the koalas would make the food in our school cafeteria seem quite tasty. They do not even come down out of their trees to drink water. In fact, they do not even drink water at all. They feed on only the leaves of the eucalyptus trees. Sometimes when they move from one particular grove of trees to another, they die because their digestive system cannot adjust.

If koalas were people, they might be called "wallflowers." If they were people, they would not be party-goers. They detest humans and stay as far away as possible from all other animals. The male koala usually keeps a small harem which he guards jealously. When infants are born, any female koala will protect (or nurse) any other infant; however, the male koala shows no interest whatsoever in his "family."

Survival for the koalas has had its ups and downs. At times they have been on the verge of extinction. Nestled quietly in the fork of a tree, the inoffensive koalas were easy targets for hunters' rifles, clubs and other weapons. They were captured for their rich fur and tender flesh. They were also starved by the destruction of the eucalyptus tree and threatened frequently by heavy brush fires. Recently the government took measures to protect them by keeping hunters from killing them and by giving them their own forest country on the east coast of Australia.

The life of koalas, either their past or present existence, would not be envied by many people. However, they have their place in the unique plan for all of human and animal existence. I'm glad I'm a person, though, instead of a koala!

CORRECTING WRITERS' ERRORS

One of the most difficult tasks for teachers of writing is deciding how to "correct" the mechanical errors made by the learners. This poses many questions:

- *Should the students' compositions be filled with "red-inked" corrections of their mistakes?*
- *Is creativity in writing **discouraged** when such errors are marked?*
- *Should the actual corrections be made by the teacher?*
- *How can the teacher ever find the **time** to mark corrections on compositions of all students' papers for every writing assignment?*
- *If the errors are marked by the teacher, how will the students learn to **identify and correct <u>their own errors</u> in their future writing?***
- *How can students be encouraged to develop and write creative and complex thoughts without being **restricted** to only those words which they can automatically spell correctly and to those sentences which they can punctuate and capitalize without error?*

The C-U-P-S System

Although these are complex questions without totally fool-proof answers, one system does offer writing instructors a workable solution. This system is called the **C-U-P-S system.** It provides a simple but effective procedure for calling each student's attention to all written mechanical errors while requiring that student to **locate** and **correct** every error.

This system works as follows:

1. Ask the students to write on alternate lines only and to leave both right and left margins empty.

2. After the first writing attempt, the teacher will write (in the left margin) the following letters to represent only the **type of error** found *in that corresponding line of writing:*

C = Capitalization error
U = Usage error
P = Punctuation error
S = Spelling error

Note that more than one of each letter may appear on the same line when multiple errors of the same type occur.

3. The papers are then returned to the students—only with letters appearing in the left margin.

4. **Each student must then <u>find and correct</u> all marked errors.** The student will make the corrections on the alternate blank lines then return the paper to the teacher.

5. The teacher will not need to reread the entire paper, but will only need to look for one correction made for each letter previously written in the left margin. The right margin may be used to place letters for errors which have either not been found or have not been corrected appropriately. See the following examples for each step in this correction process.

First Submission of Student's Writing:

	Only one of the boys were
	leaving for the halloween festivol
	Their wasn't hardly anyone going.

Instructor's First Corrections:

U	*Only one of the boys were*
CSP	*leaving for the halloween festivol*
S U	*Their wasn't hardly anyone going.*

Student's Corrected Paper:

	was
U	*Only one of the boys ~~were~~*
	Halloween festivil
CSP	*leaving for the ~~halloween~~ ~~festivol~~*
	There was
S U	*~~Their~~ ~~wasn't~~ hardly anyone going.*

Instructor's Recheck:

	was
U	*Only one of the boys ~~were~~*
	Halloween festivil S
CSP	*leaving for the ~~halloween~~ ~~festivol~~*
	There was
S U	*~~Their~~ ~~wasn't~~ hardly anyone going.*

As you use this system with your students, then train **them** to proof the papers of others before they are submitted in class.

Practice with the following student submission. In the left margin write the letter corresponding to every error in each line. (The answers appear upside down below the sample.)

Practice Sample:

	It's date is set for
	Thrusday November 20, 1994,
	which is before Thanksgiving day.
	Fourty seven seperate manu-
	scripts entitled Turkey lurkey
	will be mailed. Were you
	waiting for Jane and I to
	interview the Author.
	I said "that I was to embarassed
	to ask."

Answers: P or U (Its), S (Thursday), P (comma needed after Thursday), C (Day), S (Forty-seven), S (separate), P (title should be punctuated), C (Lurkey), U (I changed to me), C (author), P (question mark needed), P (quotation marks unneeded), S (too), S (embarrassed), P (quotation marks unneeded).

Some added thoughts:

This system may be adapted to any specific set of language rules which are taught. **Only those rules which have been discussed in class and which are expected of a particular age group should be marked.** For example, of the multitude of rules for placement of commas, only the few studied (and needed) by the learners in a fifth-grade setting should be marked on their writing samples of those fifth graders.

Additional codes for errors may be established if and when they are needed. For example, the symbol "W" may be used to indicate that a sentence or phrase needs better **W**ording, or the letters "MM" might indicate a **m**isplaced **m**odifier (such as *I sold the camera to my uncle with the flash attachment*). Any modification of a workable system should be considered.

The **teacher** does not always have to be the one to mark the mistakes. At planned times the students may exchange papers and mark the noticed errors on the papers of their classmates. A side benefit of this method is the appreciation the learners may gain of the grading chores of the teacher.

This correction system may also occur as a **group activity**, with discussions ensuing regarding changing the mistakes to their correct forms.

All errors do not always have to be marked. At some times, consider marking only the punctuation errors. On other days the capitalization errors might be indicated. The world will not end if all errors are not identified to be changed on every paper.

Do not have the students **recopy** their papers after they have corrected their mistakes. This can be highly **punitive** and can destroy any interest in future writing! On relatively infrequent occasions, each writer may wish to select a previous composition and prepare it to "show off" for an occasion (such as Family Night or for a classroom booklet). However, the papers should be considered "final" when the appropriate changes have been corrected.

EVALUATING (GRADING) STUDENTS' PAPERS

This is not any easy one! Many suggested methods for determining the final grade for students' writing creations are found in professional publications. One plan which has been encouraging to the most students is as follows:

After the learner has *corrected* the errors which are marked, then give a letter grade on the **quality of thoughts** reflected in the content of the written passage! If the thoughts in the composition were clever or creative and if the paper were concisely written, **give an "A"!** This practice is ultimately highly encouraging to quality writers. One criticism is that the final papers are not **neat.** One reaction to this is: *Who cares?* What will matter more in later years, neat papers in the classroom or a developed system of thinking through how to communicate effectively in writing? You decide!

Writing Activities

Activities for teaching writing are endless. Teachers are constantly discovering new exercises and modifying old ones. This text contains several detailed activities of varying lengths. Most are easily prepared for immediate classroom use. Some activities which are included without separate page descriptions are explained below.

The Write Right Center. Page 4 provides a design which may be photocopied and mounted on heavy colored paper to be used as a backdrop for any writing activities.

The "ME" Page. Page 14 may be used to build skills at Steps 1 and 2 in the Five-Step Writing Plan explained on page 6. This page may be photocopied and given to each separate writer. It may also be reused periodically with the same writers. At that point later thoughts may be compared with earlier (filed) examples.

Mouth Traps. Page 15 may be used to encourage anecdotal writing at Steps 4 and 5 in the Five-Step Writing Plan.

Creative Writing Cards. Getting started in the story writing process can be a major hurdle for young writers. At times a visual and verbal stimulus can be of great help. Many books which address the teaching of writing offer story starters. This text provides pages 16-24 which may be photocopied and used as desired for encouraging the writing of stories. They may be used for all steps in the Five-Step Writing Plan. Models for individual story starters may be discussed ***prior*** to the completion of the writing task.

Facts-inating Writing Cards. Pages 25-29 may encourage both factual and creative writing which relates to the content fields of science and social studies. These cards may also be photocopied for use in building Steps 4 and 5 of the Five-Step Writing Plan.

The Creative Thinking Activity. This is the only activity discussed in this text which does not have accompanying materials for immediate preparation. Because it is a favorite of many students, its explanation is included.

This exercise involves the use of several collected pictures. These pictures are pasted **inside** a file folder. A small portion of the top flap of the file folder is cut in a fashion to reveal ***only a portion of the enclosed picture.*** The writers are instructed to examine the portion of the picture which they can see. Then they are to predict what the complete picture will look like. After they write their response (usually using Steps 1, 2, or 3 of the Five-Step Writing Plan), they open the folder and compare their answer with the picture now in view.

Plastic templates may be used for ease in designing the portion of the folder to be cut. Temporary templates may be made with index cards in order to "view" what the viewing outcome might be. Below is an example of a closed and open folder for this activity.

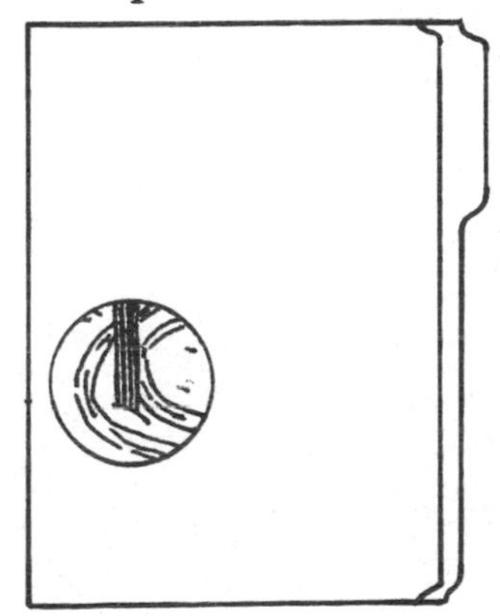

The "ME" Page

My name:
Three words which describe me best:
Three words others would use to describe me:
My best feature:
A neat expression:
My best friend:
My favorite food:
A chore I hate:
Something I wish would happen at my home:
My hero:
My favorite sport:
A car I want:
The best thing about my school:
My biggest secret:
A television character I act like:
My worst fear:
A contest I want to win:
My favorite movie star:
My heartthrob:
A political office I would like to hold:
Something I want to buy:
My chosen career:
My favorite beverage:
A place I want to visit:
A school subject I adore:
My favorite book:
A nightmare I have:
Someone I would like to have as a relative:
A movie I would like to be the star in:
Something I would like to do for my family:
A teacher I respect:
What I would do if I were in Hollywood:
A friend I would like to have:
What I would do to change our school:
My dream for America:

Mouth Traps

A Factual Writing Activity

A "Mouth Trap" is an utterance which comes out of our mouths **before** we give the words careful thought and consideration. Sometimes these utterances leave us in a trap! Almost everyone can tell a "Mouth Trap" story. Think about the times in your life when you (or someone you know) has said something which was immediately (or later) regretted. Write that story on separate paper. Below are some "Mouth Trap" examples.

Last year our teacher brought a newspaper to the classroom. She showed us a front-page story and picture of a man who had saved the life of a drowning child. She passed the newspaper around the room. As it reached me, I looked at the picture of the man.

"That's the ***ugliest*** *man I have ever seen," I said aloud before I thought.*

It was our teacher's husband.

A few years ago I had an enormous crush on a boy named Jim who sat a few rows away from me in class. Sometimes he would walk with me after school to my bus. He then walked to the parking lot where his mother picked him up. One day my bus was about an hour late. I told Jim I would walk with him to meet his mother.

As we first reached the parking lot, we saw a new expensive sports car. Jim began talking about his dream car. As we walked a little farther, I pointed to an old, beaten-up car two rows away.

"That's the ***perfect*** *car for* ***you,*** *Jim!" I loudly joked.* **That was the car he got into and rode home.**

Jim didn't walk with me to the bus after that!

When I first started to Elk School, I accidentally bumped into a girl at the water fountain.

"Watch where you are going!" I snapped, even though the bump had been my fault. I wanted the kids at my new school to know I wasn't a pushover. The girl didn't move or even look at me.

"What's the matter? Are you deaf?" I yelled even louder.

She was. *I learned a great lesson in politeness at that moment.*

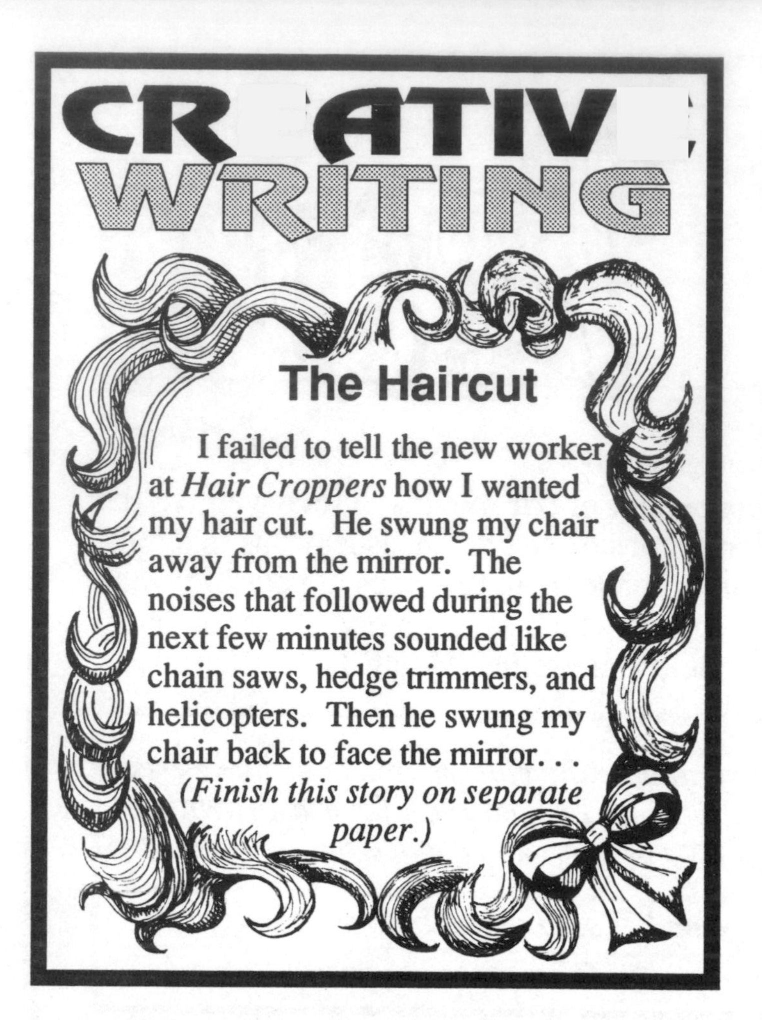

CREATIVE WRITING

The Haircut

I failed to tell the new worker at *Hair Croppers* how I wanted my hair cut. He swung my chair away from the mirror. The noises that followed during the next few minutes sounded like chain saws, hedge trimmers, and helicopters. Then he swung my chair back to face the mirror. . .

(Finish this story on separate paper.)

CREATIVE WRITING

The Pizza Substitute

I paid the delivery man from *Pizza King* and closed the front door. I placed the pizza box on the table and called my friends into the kitchen. But as I opened the box. . .

(Finish this story on separate paper.)

CREATIVE WRITING

The Goal

I've always wanted to be a football player. So I decided to try out for the UMS team. However, things didn't exactly turn out as I had wished. It all began on the day of tryouts. . .

(Finish this story on separate paper.)

CREATIVE WRITING

The Nerd

Biffy didn't start off intending to become a nerd. But suddenly one day. . .

(Finish this story on separate paper.)

CREATIVE WRITING

It's in the Bag

A bulging paper bag is lying in your driveway. You have decided to take it to your room to see what is inside. No one else is at home with you. Open this bag and describe its contents.

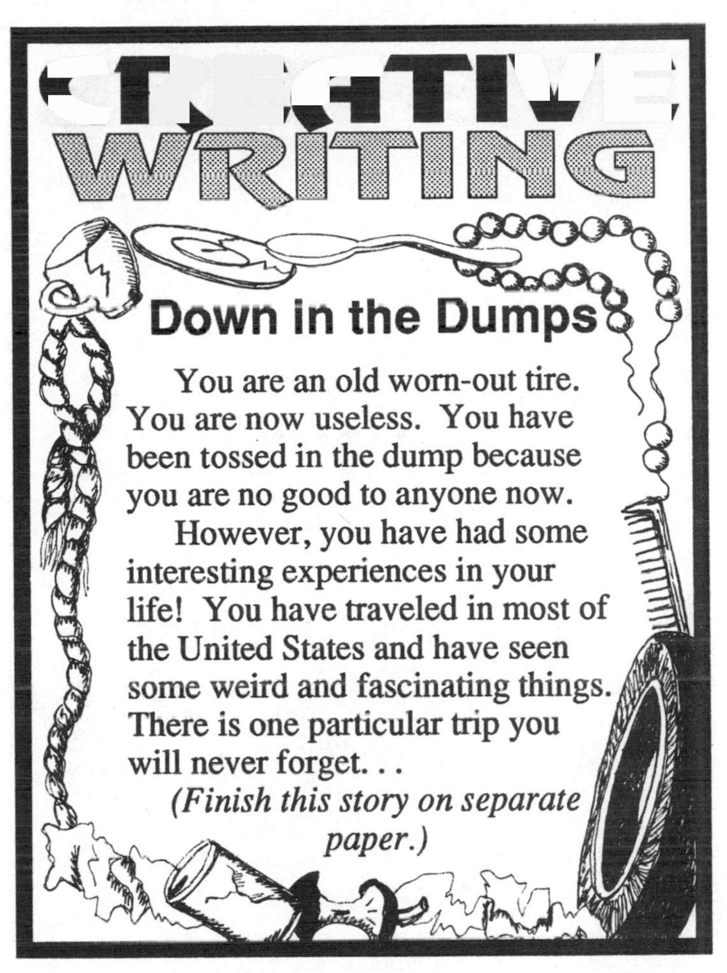

CREATIVE WRITING

Down in the Dumps

You are an old worn-out tire. You are now useless. You have been tossed in the dump because you are no good to anyone now.

However, you have had some interesting experiences in your life! You have traveled in most of the United States and have seen some weird and fascinating things. There is one particular trip you will never forget. . .

(Finish this story on separate paper.)

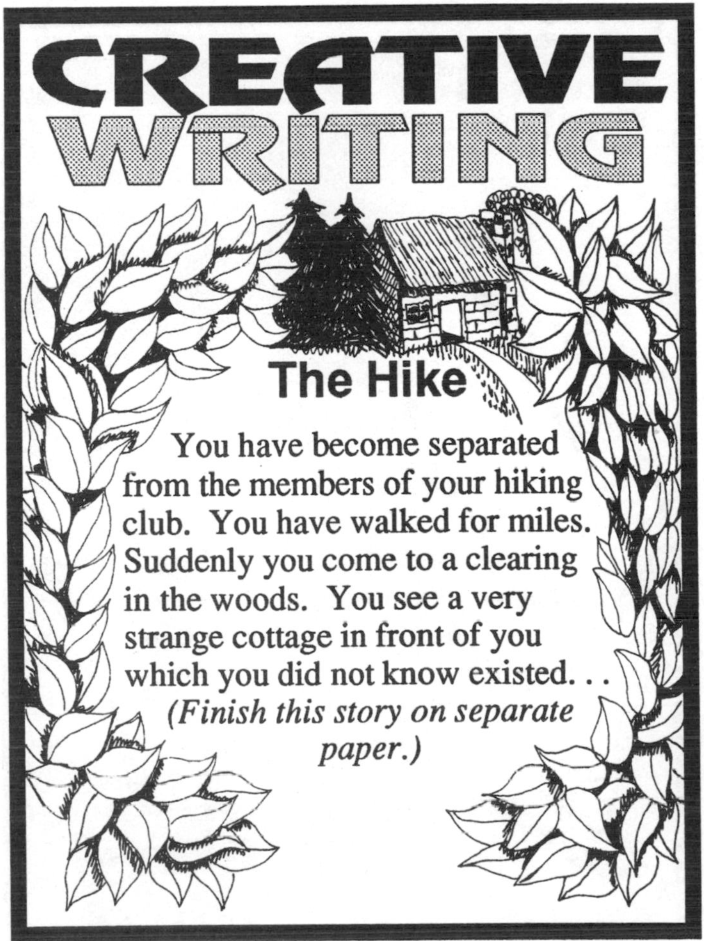

CREATIVE WRITING

The Hike

You have become separated from the members of your hiking club. You have walked for miles. Suddenly you come to a clearing in the woods. You see a very strange cottage in front of you which you did not know existed. . .

(Finish this story on separate paper.)

CREATIVE WRITING

The Animal

Susan trudged home after a long day at school. As she walked up to her front door, she noticed a very strange animal. It seemed friendly. Since no one was at home, she decided to take the animal inside. . .

(Finish this story on separate paper.)

The List

The list of people who would be invited to John's birthday party was now complete. John looked at the list.

"Oh, no," he screamed. "A name is missing! There will be **no** party unless. . .

(Finish this story on separate paper.)

The Pool Creature

You have gone outside into your backyard. You hear a noise which seems to be coming from the pool. You walk over to the pool to see a very strange creature in the water. It is alive. It is trying to say something. . .

(Finish this story on separate paper.)

The Visitor

Jan wished she had not agreed to help Tim with his homework. His voice sounded quite strange on the telephone.

"Maybe he just has a cold," she mumbled as she placed her books on the table. She had hoped her family would be home by now.

The doorbell rang. She opened the door and gasped. . .

(Finish this story on separate paper.)

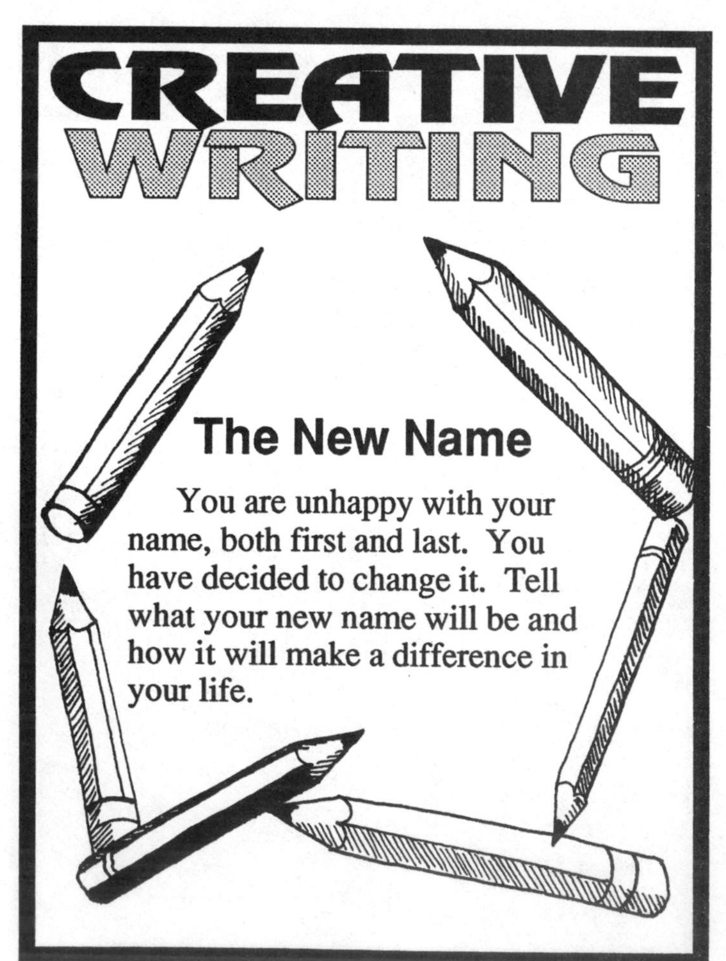

The New Name

You are unhappy with your name, both first and last. You have decided to change it. Tell what your new name will be and how it will make a difference in your life.

CREATIVE WRITING

The Alarm Clock

You have just awakened to discover that your alarm clock did not go off. It was **very** important for you to get up on time today, because. . .

(Finish this story on separate paper.)

CREATIVE WRITING

The Plane Ride

You are boarding an airplane to take your first plane ride. You are very nervous about this trip. Everyone has tried to calm you. Suddenly you hear. . .

(Finish this story on separate paper.)

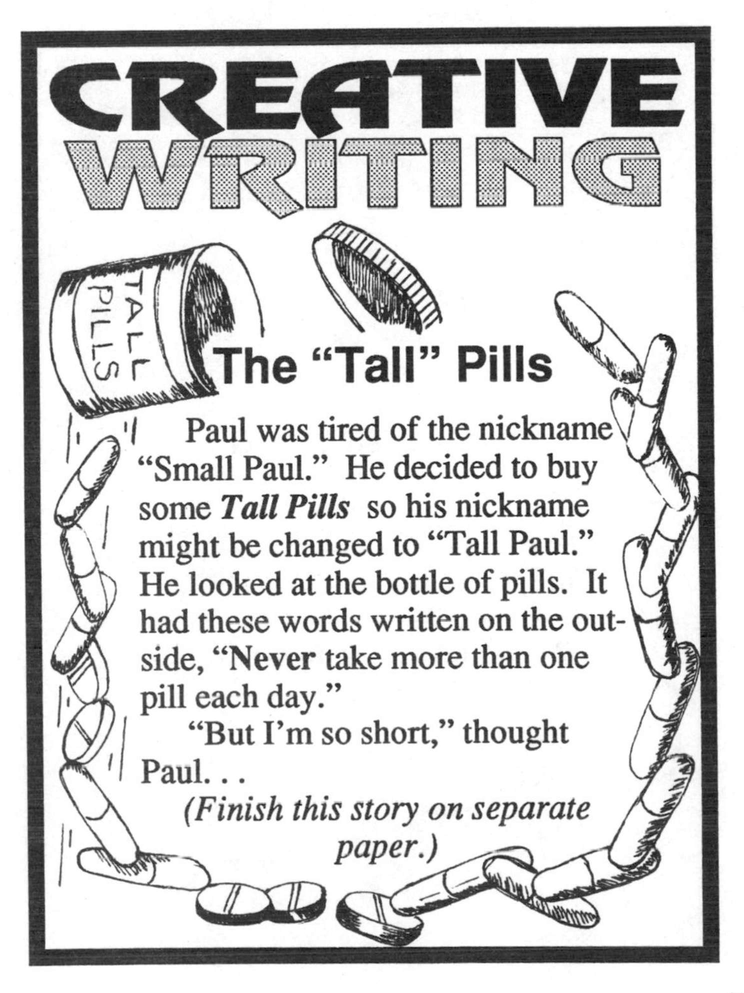

CREATIVE WRITING

The "Tall" Pills

Paul was tired of the nickname "Small Paul." He decided to buy some ***Tall Pills*** so his nickname might be changed to "Tall Paul." He looked at the bottle of pills. It had these words written on the outside, "**Never** take more than one pill each day."

"But I'm so short," thought Paul. . .

(Finish this story on separate paper.)

CREATIVE WRITING

A Glow in the Dark

A very special friend gave you a ring and asked that you wear it for the next week without taking it off. However, you placed it on the nightstand before you went to sleep. Suddenly, in the middle of the night, you notice a strange glow. It is coming from the ring. . .

(Finish this story on separate paper.)

CREATIVE WRITING

The Ride

I was the last one to leave the playground that day. On my way home a strange vehicle silently landed beside me.

"Get in!" ordered a strange-looking creature.

Suddenly a force started pulling me toward the vehicle. . .

(Finish this story on separate paper.)

CREATIVE WRITING

The Picnic Basket

Sam and Sue left their picnic basket in the woods while they went to pick some berries. About an hour later they returned, eager to have lunch. But as they opened the basket. . .

(Finish this story on separate paper.)

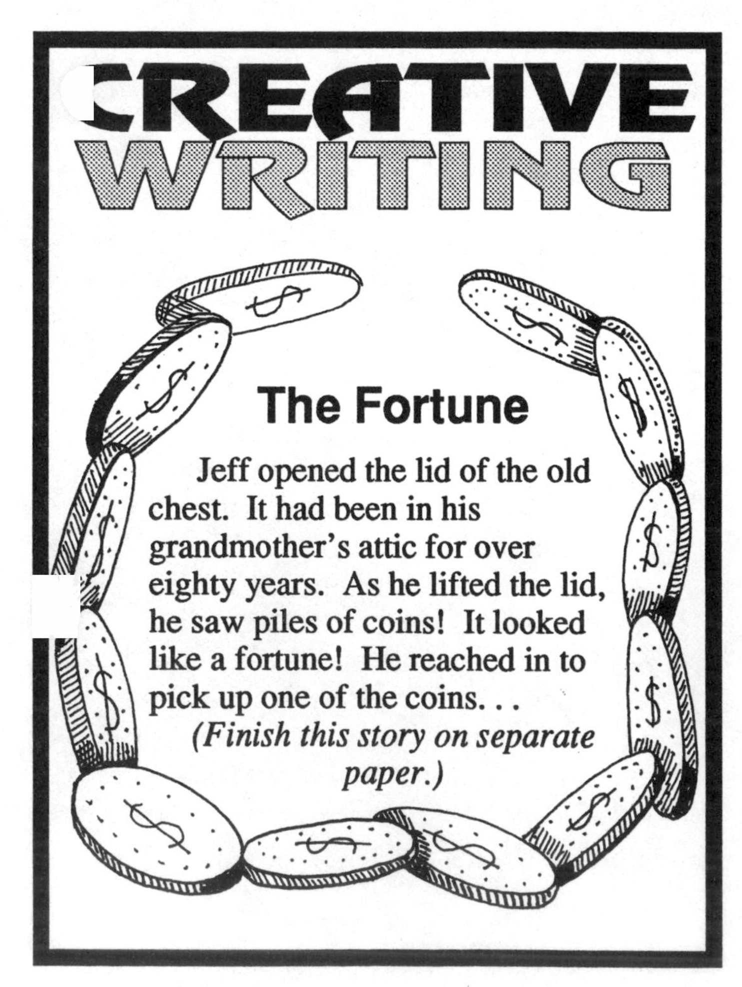

CREATIVE WRITING

The Fortune

Jeff opened the lid of the old chest. It had been in his grandmother's attic for over eighty years. As he lifted the lid, he saw piles of coins! It looked like a fortune! He reached in to pick up one of the coins. . .

(Finish this story on separate paper.)

CREATIVE WRITING

The Matches

Mother had told Lou not to play with matches. Lou generally did as her mother asked. But one day. . .

(Finish this story on separate paper.)

CREATIVE WRITING

The Telegram

"I have a telegram for Lee Jones," announced the delivery man.

"That's for me," Lee answered.

"Sign here," he said nervously.

Lee slowly opened the telegram and began reading. . .

(Finish this story on separate paper.)

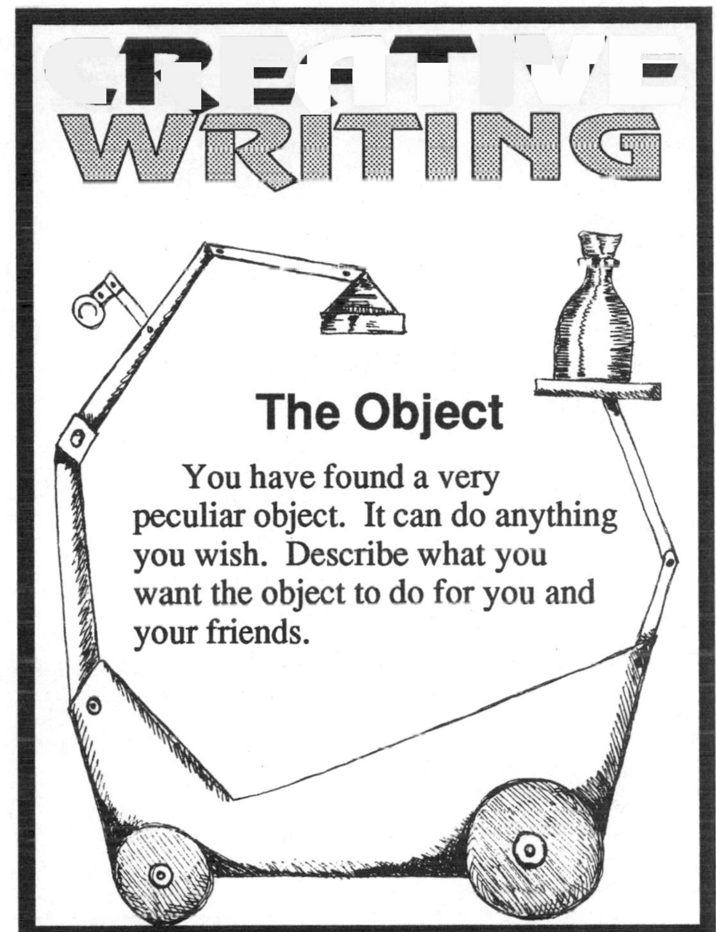

CREATIVE WRITING

The Object

You have found a very peculiar object. It can do anything you wish. Describe what you want the object to do for you and your friends.

CREATIVE WRITING

The Cave

"I wouldn't go into that cave if I were you," Jason explained to Mark. "You heard what happened to the last three people who did!"

"That doesn't scare me at all. Besides, we have no **proof** of what happened to the others. So **I'm** going **in**," said Mark.

Mark boldly stepped inside the cave. . .

(Finish this story on separate paper.)

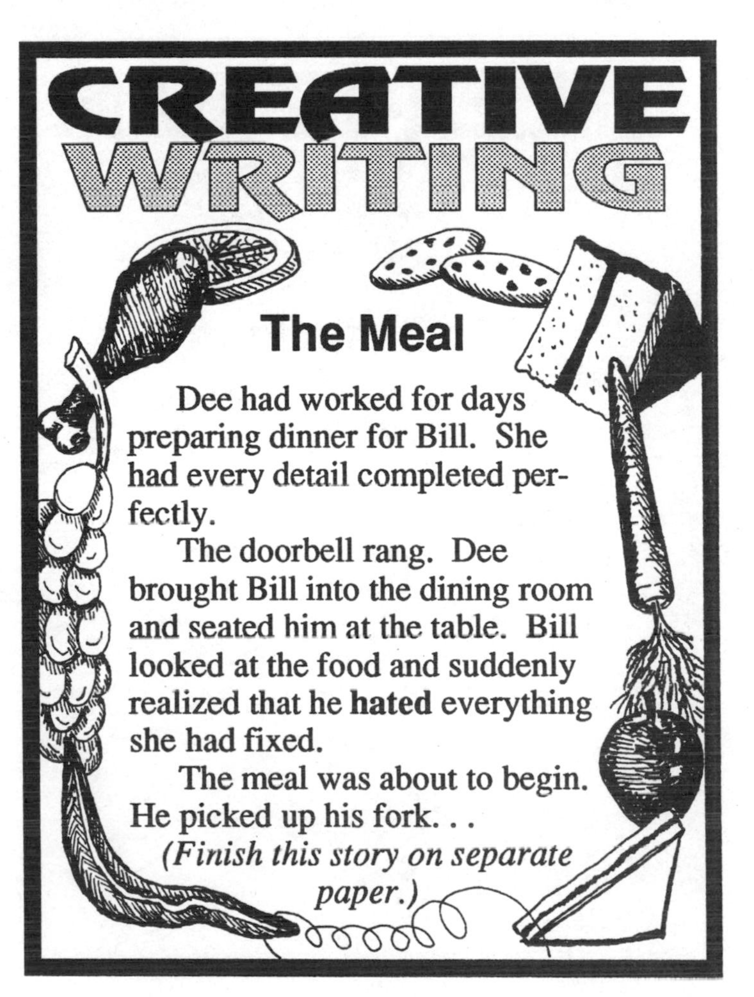

CREATIVE WRITING

The Meal

Dee had worked for days preparing dinner for Bill. She had every detail completed perfectly.

The doorbell rang. Dee brought Bill into the dining room and seated him at the table. Bill looked at the food and suddenly realized that he **hated** everything she had fixed.

The meal was about to begin. He picked up his fork. . .

(Finish this story on separate paper.)

CREATIVE WRITING

I'm Outstanding!

If you were ever in the future going to be listed in the *Book of Outstanding World Records*, what would you want your accomplishments to be? After you think about this, prepare your entry as you hope it would appear. Use real names and dates.

CREATIVE WRITING

School Records

Write a story which you think could appear in *The Book of World Records for School Happenings*. Do not use real names, but base your story on at least **one** fact.

CREATIVE WRITING

It's Ridiculous

A new book will be published next year entitled *The Book of Ridiculous Records*. These stories will report a variety of ridiculous happenings, such as the number of marshmallows stuffed in one mouth without chewing or swallowing. Write a ridiculous story for this new book. It does not need to be based on fact.

CREATIVE WRITING

The Menace

Someone in your family or neighborhood is writing *The Menace Book of World Records*. The editor is looking for stories to include. Write a story which you think should appear in this book. Do not use real names.

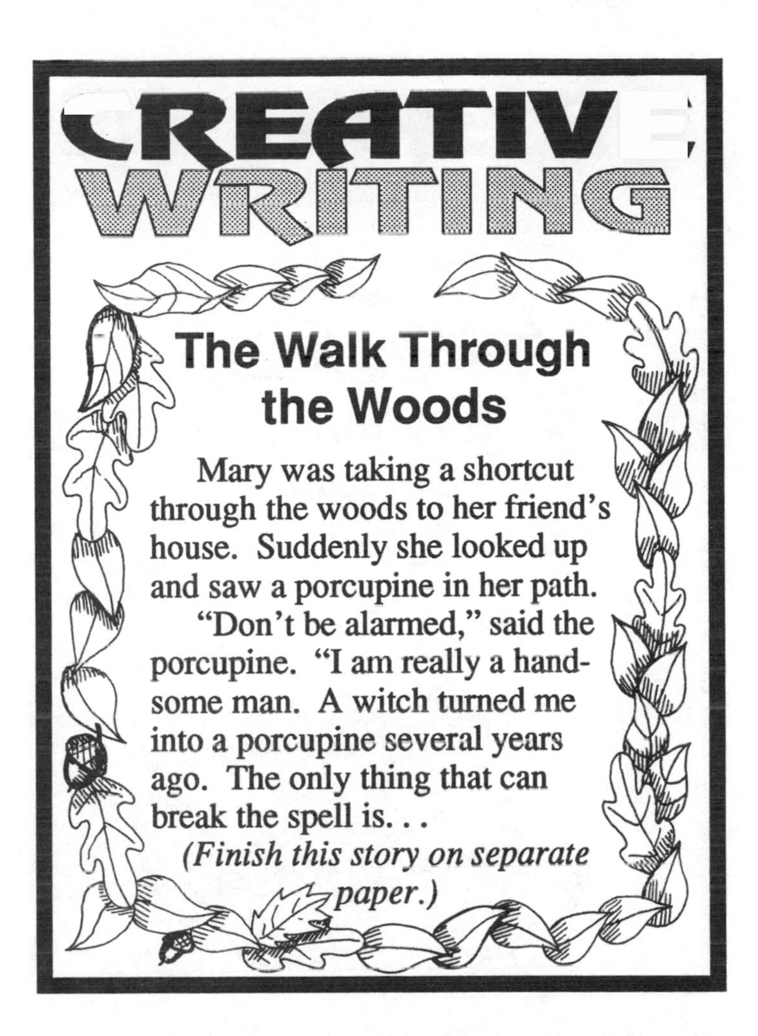

CREATIVE WRITING

The Walk Through the Woods

Mary was taking a shortcut through the woods to her friend's house. Suddenly she looked up and saw a porcupine in her path.

"Don't be alarmed," said the porcupine. "I am really a handsome man. A witch turned me into a porcupine several years ago. The only thing that can break the spell is. . .

(Finish this story on separate paper.)

CREATIVE WRITING

The Flood

The water was rising faster and faster. It was now above my waist. I knew it would be almost impossible for someone to rescue me. I tried to loosen the ropes which bound my ankles and wrists. . .

(Finish this story on separate paper.)

CREATIVE WRITING

The Masked Man

I was running fast to try to escape. As I rounded the corner, I was face to face with a masked man. . .

(Finish this story on separate paper.)

CREATIVE WRITING

The Loaded Gun

I didn't know the gun was loaded. Daddy had always left guns unloaded. I had thought it would be fun to pretend. . .

(Finish this story on separate paper.)

The Creep

The doorbell was ringing. I could see it was "The Creep." I didn't want to open the door, especially after what happened yesterday. . .

(Finish this story on separate paper.)

The Midnight Scream

It was bloodcurdling!
It was terrifying!
It brought chillbumps to all in the neighborhood!
It was midnight. . .

(Finish this story on separate paper.)

The Cellar Surprise

"Go down into the cellar and bring me that old broom Uncle George left here last summer," Mom yelled.

"I don't like going into our cellar, Mom," I snapped. "It's so spooky!"

"I need it **now**!" she demanded.

I knew she meant business. I walked to the cellar door, opened it, and slowly descended. . .

(Finish this story on separate paper.)

Help!

When I realized what was happening, I began to panic. The sounds of my own heartbeat seemed louder than actual thunder. I knew I must call for help. But as I opened my mouth. . .

(Finish this story on separate paper.)

Facts-inating Writing: Rodents and Felines

Facts-inating Writing: Rodents and Felines Card 1

Fact: The teeth of rodents continue to grow throughout their entire lives. They remain worn down, however, through their constant gnawing. (Rodents are gnawing or nibbling mammals such as mice, rats, squirrels or beavers.)
Fiction: If human teeth continued to grow, describe a new occupation which might be needed. Explain an imaginary daily routine of one in such a profession.

Facts-inating Writing: Rodents and Felines Card 2

Fact: The taste buds of felines do not detect sweetness. (Felines are mammals belonging to the cat family.)
Fiction: Design a fancy dessert for a cat. Explain your choice of ingredients.

Facts-inating Writing: Rodents and Felines Card 3

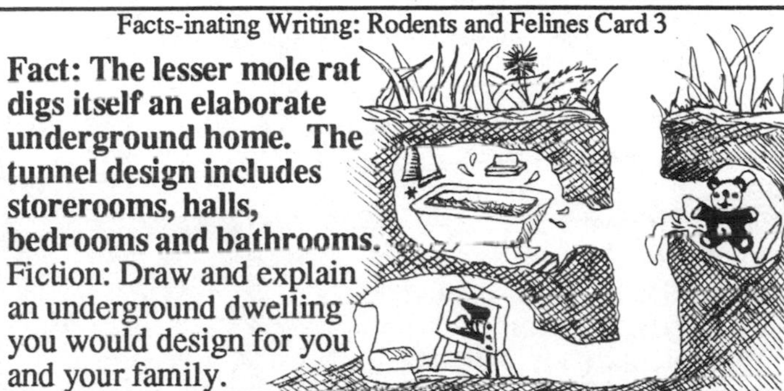

Fact: The lesser mole rat digs itself an elaborate underground home. The tunnel design includes storerooms, halls, bedrooms and bathrooms.
Fiction: Draw and explain an underground dwelling you would design for you and your family.

Facts-inating Writing: Rodents and Felines Card 4

Fact: A cat uses its whiskers to tell if a space is large enough to crawl through. If the whiskers (which serve as "feelers") touch at either side, the space is too small.
Fiction: If a cat accidentally got its whiskers trimmed, describe one "tight spot" it could possibly experience.

Facts-inating Writing: Rodents and Felines Card 5

Kangaroo rats drink no water at all. They turn the air they breathe and the dry food they eat into water. Using their special kidneys, they recycle their body's water content, thus preventing water loss.
Fiction: If YOU could drink no water at all for one month, describe a plan you would use in order to stay alive.

Facts-inating Writing: Rodents and Felines Card 6

Fact: A rat can jump from a five-story building without harm.
Fiction: Describe one way it might be possible for a human to jump from the fifth floor of a building without injury.

Facts-inating Writing: Rodents and Felines Card 7

Fact: One method of protection for a cat is its appearance. It can cause its fur to stand up, thus looking twice its normal size. It arches its back and raises its haunches to appear tall and powerful.
Fiction: Describe one way YOUR APPEARANCE can cause you to look more powerful.

Facts-inating Writing: Rodents and Felines Card 8

Fact: The squirrel sees only in black and white.
Fiction: Some people are also color-blind in varying degrees. Explain one problem which could be encountered by a person who is completely color-blind.

Facts-inating Writing: Rodents and Felines Card 9

Fact: The puma (a large feline) can do a broad jump of forty feet (122 m).
Fiction: Measure a distance of forty feet (122 m). Describe a situation when you might need to jump that distance. What might the outcome be at that time?

Facts-inating Writing: Rodents and Felines Card 10

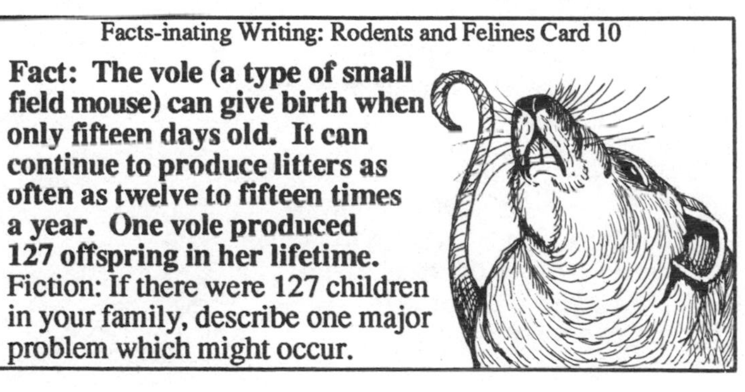

Fact: The vole (a type of small field mouse) can give birth when only fifteen days old. It can continue to produce litters as often as twelve to fifteen times a year. One vole produced 127 offspring in her lifetime.
Fiction: If there were 127 children in your family, describe one major problem which might occur.

Facts-inating Writing: Heads Up!

Facts-inating Writing: Heads Up! Card 1

Fact: The human brain is the approximate size of a large grapefruit. The stegosaurus, an extinct giant dinosaur, had a brain no larger than a walnut.
Fiction: If you could have talked with a stegosaurus, describe one conversation you might have had.

Facts-inating Writing: Heads Up! Card 2

Fact: As long as one lives, the nose and ears continue to increase in size.
Fiction: If medical researchers learn how to extend the average life span to 200 years, describe a new problem the elderly might "face" because of the above fact.

Facts-inating Writing: Heads Up! Card 3

Fact: After the Battle of Waterloo, many dentures were made from teeth extracted from the corpses of soldiers on the Waterloo battlefield.
Fiction: You have just been fitted with a set of "Waterloo" teeth. Something strange is beginning to happen to you, especially when you talk. Describe one weird conversation you might have.

Facts-inating Writing: Heads Up! Card 4

Fact: Noises, even mild or faint ones, cause the pupils of the eyes to dilate. Noises cause the pupils to change focus and can temporarily blur vision.
Fiction: Explain the problems a surgeon might have if the Rock Banned Band moves in next door to the operating room. (YOU are the patient!)

Facts-inating Writing: Heads Up! Card 5

Fact: Human hair is practically impossible to destroy. It is extremely slow to disintegrate, is not destroyed by climate or natural forces, and resists most acids and corrosive chemicals.
Fiction: You are the owner of The Happy Hair Salon. You have decided to put the cut human hair to use. Explain one plan you have.

Facts-inating Writing: Heads Up! Card 6

Fact: All people have tongue prints as unique as their fingerprints.
Fiction: You are a famous detective. You have just finished a case where the tongue print was the crucial factor in the solution of a crime. Describe this case.

Facts-inating Writing: Heads Up! Card 7

Fact: People cannot sneeze with their eyes open.
Fiction: You have just entered the Million Dollar Watch. In front of you is a video monitor. You will win a million dollars if you activate a designated switch within one second after a red flash appears on the monitor. As the clock is ticking, you feel a sneeze approaching. Explain what you will do.

Facts-inating Writing: Heads Up! Card 8

Fact: One cannot taste food AT ALL, even flavors such as salt or sugar, until it is mixed with saliva.
Fiction: Explain one situation where being unable to taste food might be advantageous to someone.

Facts-inating Writing: Heads Up! Card 9

Fact: About seven percent of males have some form of color blindness. Most of these experience difficulties with shades of red and green.
Fiction: Claude Santers is color-blind. He has just been hired to be Santa Claus for the local mall. Describe one problem he may experience.

Facts-inating Writing: Heads Up! Card 10

Fact: Forty-three muscles are used to frown. Seventeen are used to smile.
Fiction: You have been appointed as chairman of the Smile League for your school. Using the above facts, design a smile poster to solicit members for your group.

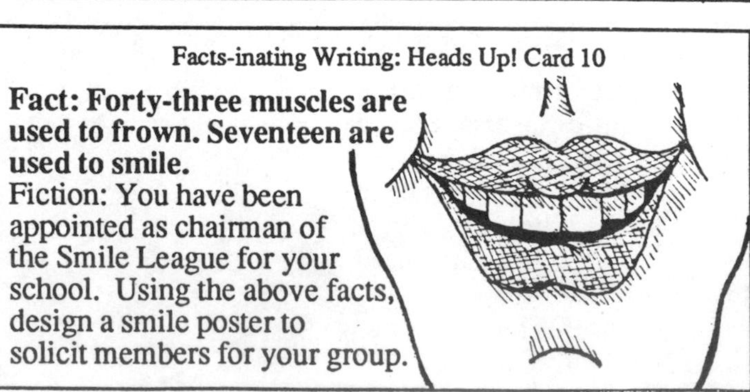

Facts-inating Writing: Bodacious Birds

Facts-inating Writing: Bodacious Birds Card 1

Fact: One ostrich egg is large enough to make an omelette for twelve people. It may take at least two hours to hard-boil an ostrich egg.
Fiction: If you were a cook for a large restaurant and could use eggs only from the ostrich, make up one funny situation which might possibly occur.

Facts-inating Writing: Bodacious Birds Card 2

Fact: The myna bird can repeat human sounds with an amazing degree of accuracy. One myna bird owner got rid of his bird after hearing it constantly repeat his own outbursts.
Fiction: If you owned a myna bird, it could mimic much of what you say. Relate a story you would definitely not want your myna bird to repeat to your friends.

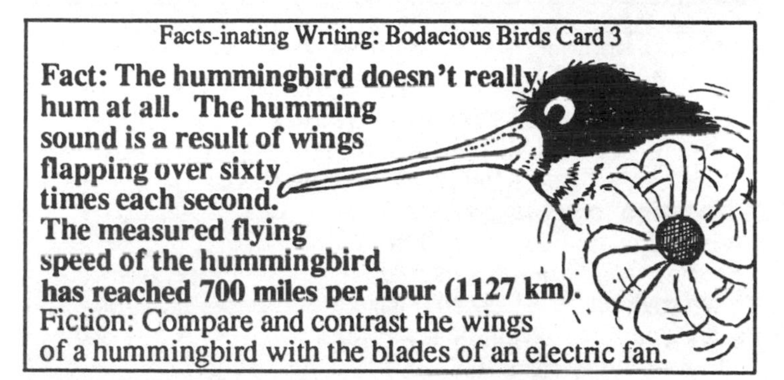

Facts-inating Writing: Bodacious Birds Card 3

Fact: The hummingbird doesn't really hum at all. The humming sound is a result of wings flapping over sixty times each second. The measured flying speed of the hummingbird has reached 700 miles per hour (1127 km).
Fiction: Compare and contrast the wings of a hummingbird with the blades of an electric fan.

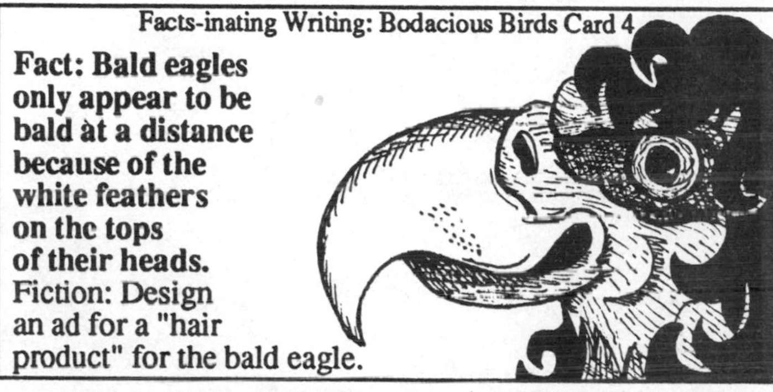

Facts-inating Writing: Bodacious Birds Card 4

Fact: Bald eagles only appear to be bald at a distance because of the white feathers on the tops of their heads.
Fiction: Design an ad for a "hair product" for the bald eagle.

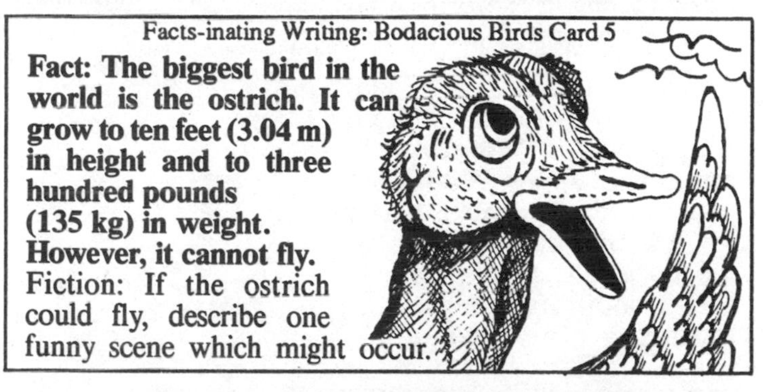

Facts-inating Writing: Bodacious Birds Card 5

Fact: The biggest bird in the world is the ostrich. It can grow to ten feet (3.04 m) in height and to three hundred pounds (135 kg) in weight. However, it cannot fly.
Fiction: If the ostrich could fly, describe one funny scene which might occur.

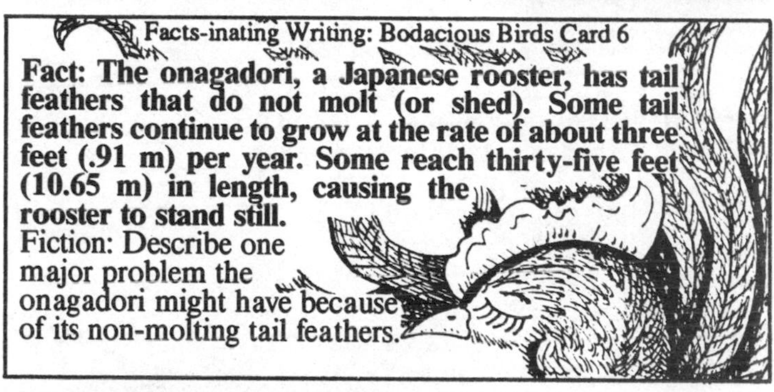

Facts-inating Writing: Bodacious Birds Card 6

Fact: The onagadori, a Japanese rooster, has tail feathers that do not molt (or shed). Some tail feathers continue to grow at the rate of about three feet (.91 m) per year. Some reach thirty-five feet (10.65 m) in length, causing the rooster to stand still.
Fiction: Describe one major problem the onagadori might have because of its non-molting tail feathers.

Facts-inating Writing: Bodacious Birds Card 7

Fact: The Arctic tern makes a round-trip migratory flight of 22,000 miles each year.
Fiction: Write a diary entry of one day in a migratory flight from the viewpoint of an Arctic tern.

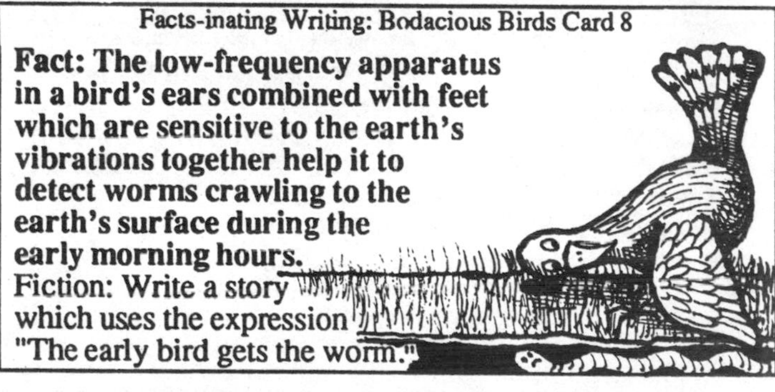

Facts-inating Writing: Bodacious Birds Card 8

Fact: The low-frequency apparatus in a bird's ears combined with feet which are sensitive to the earth's vibrations together help it to detect worms crawling to the earth's surface during the early morning hours.
Fiction: Write a story which uses the expression "The early bird gets the worm."

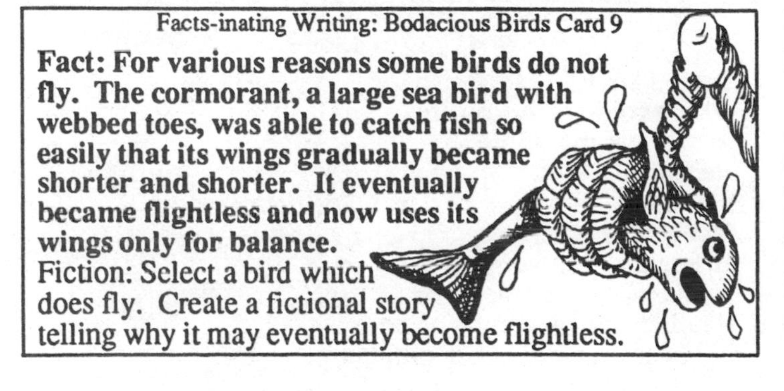

Facts-inating Writing: Bodacious Birds Card 9

Fact: For various reasons some birds do not fly. The cormorant, a large sea bird with webbed toes, was able to catch fish so easily that its wings gradually became shorter and shorter. It eventually became flightless and now uses its wings only for balance.
Fiction: Select a bird which does fly. Create a fictional story telling why it may eventually become flightless.

Facts-inating Writing: Bodacious Birds Card 10

Fact: Birds do not have teeth. Their stomachs vigorously agitate the many hard substances swallowed before passing them through the digestive tract.
Fiction: Describe one major problem you might have if you had no teeth.

Facts-inating Writing: Prestigious Presidents

Facts-inating Writing: Prestigious Presidents Card 1

Fact: Because of the tragic death of his fiancée, JAMES BUCHANAN (1857-1861) never married. While he was President, his niece served as First Lady.

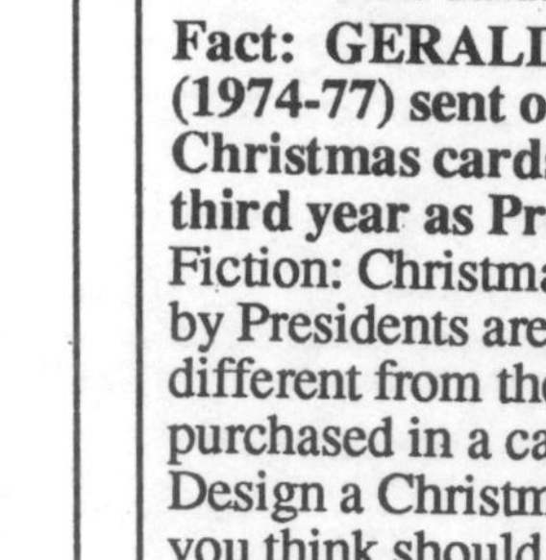

Fiction: If you were an unmarried United States President, tell whom you would select to serve as your First Lady/Gentleman. Explain your choice.

Facts-inating Writing: Prestigious Presidents Card 2

Fact: GERALD R. FORD (1974-77) sent over 40,000 Christmas cards during his third year as President.

Fiction: Christmas cards sent by Presidents are generally different from those purchased in a card shop. Design a Christmas card which you think should be sent by a President.

Facts-inating Writing: Prestigious Presidents Card 3

Fact: During his term as President, ULYSSES S. GRANT (1869-1877) was arrested for speeding while on his horse. His horse and rig were impounded, and the President walked home.

Fiction: Describe an appropriate punishment for a President who is caught speeding on a horse.

Facts-inating Writing: Prestigious Presidents Card 4

Fact: WILLIAM McKINLEY (1897-1901) thought that wearing a red carnation would bring him good luck. It became his trademark. One fall at a New York fairground McKinley gave away his carnation to young Myrtle Krass. An hour later he was assassinated.

Fiction: Many famous people have trademarks. Describe a trademark you think might be appropriate for our current President. Explain your choice.

Facts-inating Writing: Prestigious Presidents Card 5

Fact: "S" was HARRY S TRUMAN'S (1945-1953) middle name. The use of a single letter as a middle name was an early common practice in the United States and England. This letter was considered correctly written without a period.

Fiction: If you had a single letter of the alphabet as a middle name, tell which letter you would choose and why.

Facts-inating Writing: Prestigious Presidents Card 6

Fact: A President must shake hands often. One New Year's Day, THEODORE ROOSEVELT (1901-1909) shook hands with almost 9000 people.

Fiction: Tennis elbow is a name given to an irritation caused by playing tennis. Create a name for a condition resulting in shaking too many hands in one day. Offer a remedy for such an ailment.

Facts-inating Writing: Prestigious Presidents Card 7

Fact: Richard Lawrence was the first person to attempt the assassination of a United States President. While only six feet (1.82 m) away from ANDREW JACKSON (1829-1837), Lawrence aimed his pistol and pulled the trigger. The gun misfired. Lawrence drew another loaded gun, aimed, and pulled the trigger. The second gun also misfired. The odds of this happening are one in one hundred thousand.

Fiction: Describe an appropriate punishment for someone who attempts to assassinate a President.

Facts-inating Writing: Prestigious Presidents Card 8

Fact: ZACHARY TAYLOR (1849-1850) was sixty-two when he first voted. He did not even vote in his own election.

Fiction: Many people of voting age today choose not to vote. They give many excuses for not exercising this American privilege. Select an excuse which might be given by a nonvoter; then present an argument against using such an excuse.

Facts-inating Writing: Prestigious Presidents Card 9

Fact: While serving as President, JOHN QUINCY ADAMS (1824-1829) went "skinny dipping" in the Potomac River every summer morning around 4 a.m.

Fiction: During the time Adams was President, such an activity was considered a healthy physical exercise. It was also treated as Adams' own personal business. However, if today's President did such an exercise, describe how reporters might treat such an event.

Facts-inating Writing: Prestigious Presidents Card 10

Fact: JAMES GARFIELD (1881) could write Latin with one hand while writing Greek with the other.

Fiction: Describe two different activities you would like to be able to do simultaneously—one with your right hand and the other with your left.

Facts-inating Writing: Intriguing Insects

Facts-inating Writing: Intriguing Insects Card 1

Fact: The South American cucuyo beetle has two "headlights" on its thorax which produce lights bright enough that it is possible to read a book by them.
Fiction: Several cucuyo beetles are inquiring about books for "night reading." Suggest three books (real or imaginary) for them to read. Give reasons for each selection.

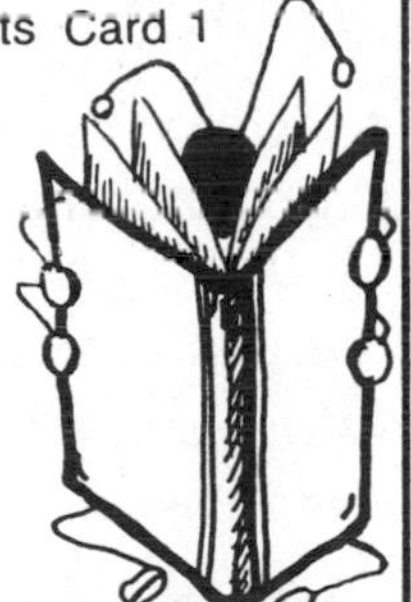

Facts-inating Writing: Intriguing Insects Card 2

Fact: On the average (in the United States) there are only five deaths per year from wasps and five from bees. Seventeen-month-old Mark Bennet once survived 447 wasp stings.
Fiction: Describe one possible reaction Mark might have toward wasps in his later years.

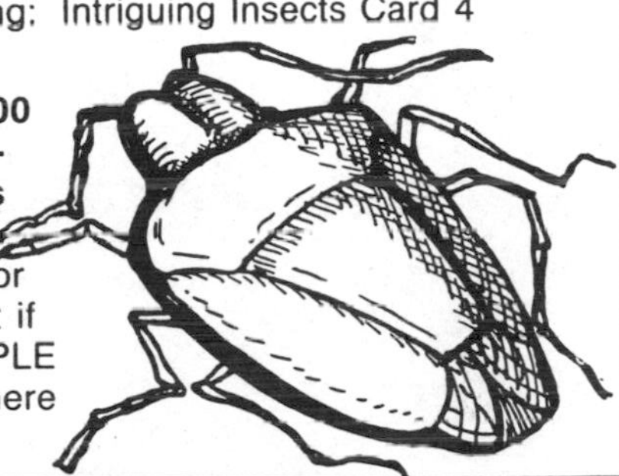

Facts-inating Writing: Intriguing Insects Card 3

Fact: A bombardier beetle can defend itself by making noises similar to popgun blasts and by ejecting a red cloud of foul-smelling liquid.
Fiction: The neighborhood bully is out to get you. Describe an unusual defense you would like to create for your protection against this bully.

Facts-inating Writing: Intriguing Insects Card 4

Fact: There are over 1,000,000,000,000,000,000 (one quintillion) living insects in the world at this moment.
Fiction: Describe one major problem which might exist if there were as many PEOPLE living on Earth today as there are insects.

Facts-inating Writing: Intriguing Insects Card 5

Fact: A bee can lift or drag objects 300 times its own weight.
Fiction: If people could physically do this same thing, describe one way society might be different.

Facts-inating Writing: Intriguing Insects Card 6

Fact: When ants awaken, they stretch and yawn in much the same manner as humans do.
Fiction: If people decided to mimic some behaviors of ants, describe one humorous situation which might occur.

Facts-inating Writing: Intriguing Insects Card 7

Fact: Cockroaches can continue living (sometimes for several weeks) after their heads have been cut off.
Fiction: Several dozen headless cockroaches are in your basement. Describe a game they might play to amuse themselves.

Facts-inating Writing: Intriguing Insects Card 8

Fact: Most grasshoppers can jump over obstacles up to 500 times their own height.
Fiction: Determine how high you would be able to jump if you had the same leaping ability as the grasshopper. Describe one experience you would like to have.

Facts-inating Writing: Intriguing Insects Card 9

Fact: A single pair of flies could produce 190,000,000,000,000,000,000 offspring in four months if all survived.
Fiction: If this many flies DID survive, explain one clever solution for helping to get rid of them.

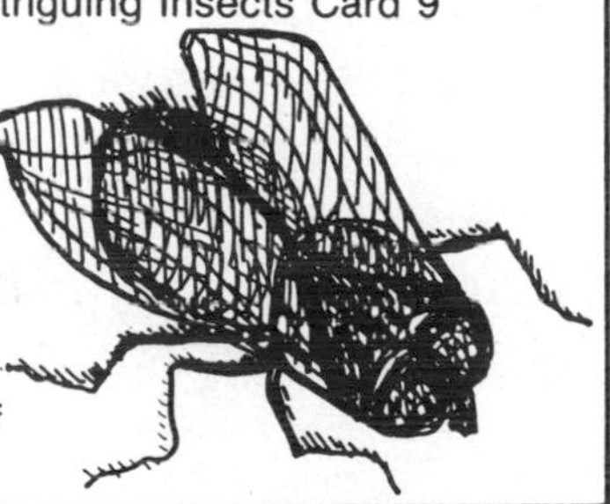

Facts-inating Writing: Intriguing Insects Card 10

Fact: The deer botfly can fly at a speed of over 800 miles (1288 km) per hour.
Fiction: If YOU were able to fly at this speed, describe one trip you would like to take.

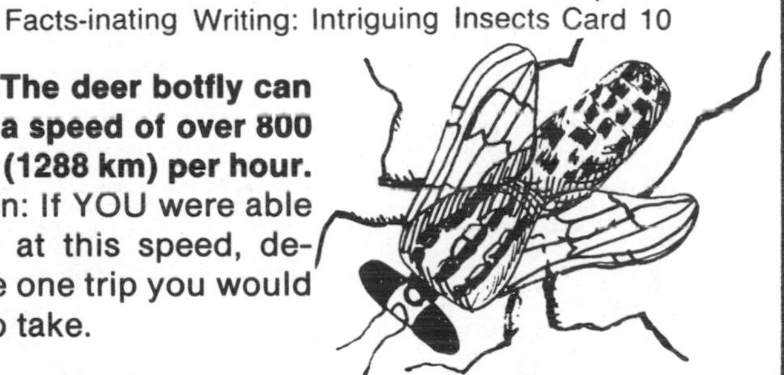

Personal Worth Notes

Personal Worth Notes is a unique activity which combines factual and creative writing experiences. The following are suggestions for the preparation and use of this activity.

1. Make one copy of the bill on the following page for each participant. (Although this is not the side of the bill which is printed with green ink, these photocopies may be run on green paper for a special visual effect.) Bills which are to be reused may be laminated or covered with clear self-adhesive paper, if desired.

Request a small photograph of each participant. For each student cut an oval large enough for the head shot of the corresponding photograph. This may be as small as the white area or may include any or all of the outer shaded oval.

Tape the pictures of the students **behind** these openings in the bills. Write the names in the long white rectangular area below the ovals.

Ask each student to write a paragraph about his or her own personal worth. (Encourage emphases in nonmonetary areas.)

Bills with notes may be displayed on bulletin board or wall areas.

2. Proceed as suggested in Step 1 with the preparation of the bills. Instead of using pictures of students, use pictures of famous people. Have learners write about what they think these individuals are worth. Again, discourage writing about monetary factors only.

3. Use a picture of the classroom teacher, the school principal, or other school or community leader.

4. Use pictures of objects or food which may be of importance to the writers. A question may be written in the rectangular area. An example might be a **hamburger,** with the question, "Of what value to you (or to America) is the hamburger?"

5. Use any other types of pictures or objects which might provide an appropriate stimulus for good writing experiences.

6. The above suggestions pertain to writing experiences for individual learners. Any or all of them may also be used as group activities. Arrange students into small groups of three to five. Give the entire group one picture (especially from suggestions 2-5 above. Have the entire group brainstorm for a final written passage, or have the brainstorming result in a written product from each separate group member.

PERSONAL WORTH NOTES
UNITED EFFORTS
THIS PERSONAL NOTE IS NOT LEGAL AND IT IS VERY TOUGH.
JOY
I M A U-MB-N ! R U ?
Cut out this white area (or a larger oval). Tape any picture or photo behind the cut area. Write student's name/product title in the rectangle below.
S, I M A U-MB-N ! U R 2 !
I'M NO.
ONE
Secretary of Nothing

THE ADVENTURE

Writing activities may appear in game board fashion. **The Adventure** is a series of boards which may be used to encourage unusual writing creations.

Preparation of Boards

Pages 33-41 may be photocopied from this book onto heavy, colorful paper. If such paper is not available, regular copies may be used and mounted onto heavier paper. If desired, these boards may be protected with laminating film or clear self-adhesive paper. A spinner will need to be attached to each board with a paper fastener. (**Loosely** attach these paper fasteners.) The boards are now ready to use. Page 42 may be used for students to create new boards.

Writing Activities

A variety of writing activities may occur with these boards. For an individual writing experience, each writer may spin one board at a time and make notes of the items on which the spinners landed. That writer then creates a story which incorporates every spun item. An example of a collection of spun items is as follows: *a beaver, a cobra, an owl, a mosquito, a hammock, a pillow, thermal socks, bubble gum, and a motorcycle.*

Adaptations of the above writing suggestions may offer interest and variety. Instead of individual writers, groupings of any desired size may occur. Rather than each writer spinning separately, one person may spin for everyone. The items selected may then be written on the chalkboard for all to include in their written responses. For another variation, each writer may **select** rather than spin the items shown on each board. The writers themselves may suggest other uses of these boards.

Each level of the Five-Step Writing Plan (explained on page 6) may be developed through the use of these boards. The procedure above describes the concepts involved in Step 5. Earlier steps may be taught **prior** to the writing of these final stories. An example would be to spin any one board (such as **Animal Choices**) and ask for a word which would describe that animal. If **zebra** were chosen, words such as *striped, big,* or *nondomestic* might be offered. This step could proceed into the writing of phrases, sentences, and paragraphs. Finally, the writers create a complete story incorporating several different concepts in the plot.

Models for writing such longer selections may also be discussed. Although every final product will be different both in content and structure, a generic model may be discussed. One such model might be as follows: *Story introduction (includes setting description), a proposed conflict, first event, remaining happenings (each step in the plot development may be in a separate paragraph), the solution of the conflict, and the story conclusion.*

Proceed with such activities which meet the writing needs and desires of the group involved.

Note that the items to be spun on these provided boards have both pictures and matching words as choices. In this manner students who have spelling difficulties may <u>copy</u> the words at the edges of the boards. Also it allows nonreaders to use these boards as an activity for oral expression. These included selections also show pictorial representations which are factually accurate. This is intentionally presented in this manner for the purpose of increasing the student's knowledge base in these selected categories. Many factual writing experiences may also be designed from these pages.

THE ADVENTURE

ANIMAL CHOICES

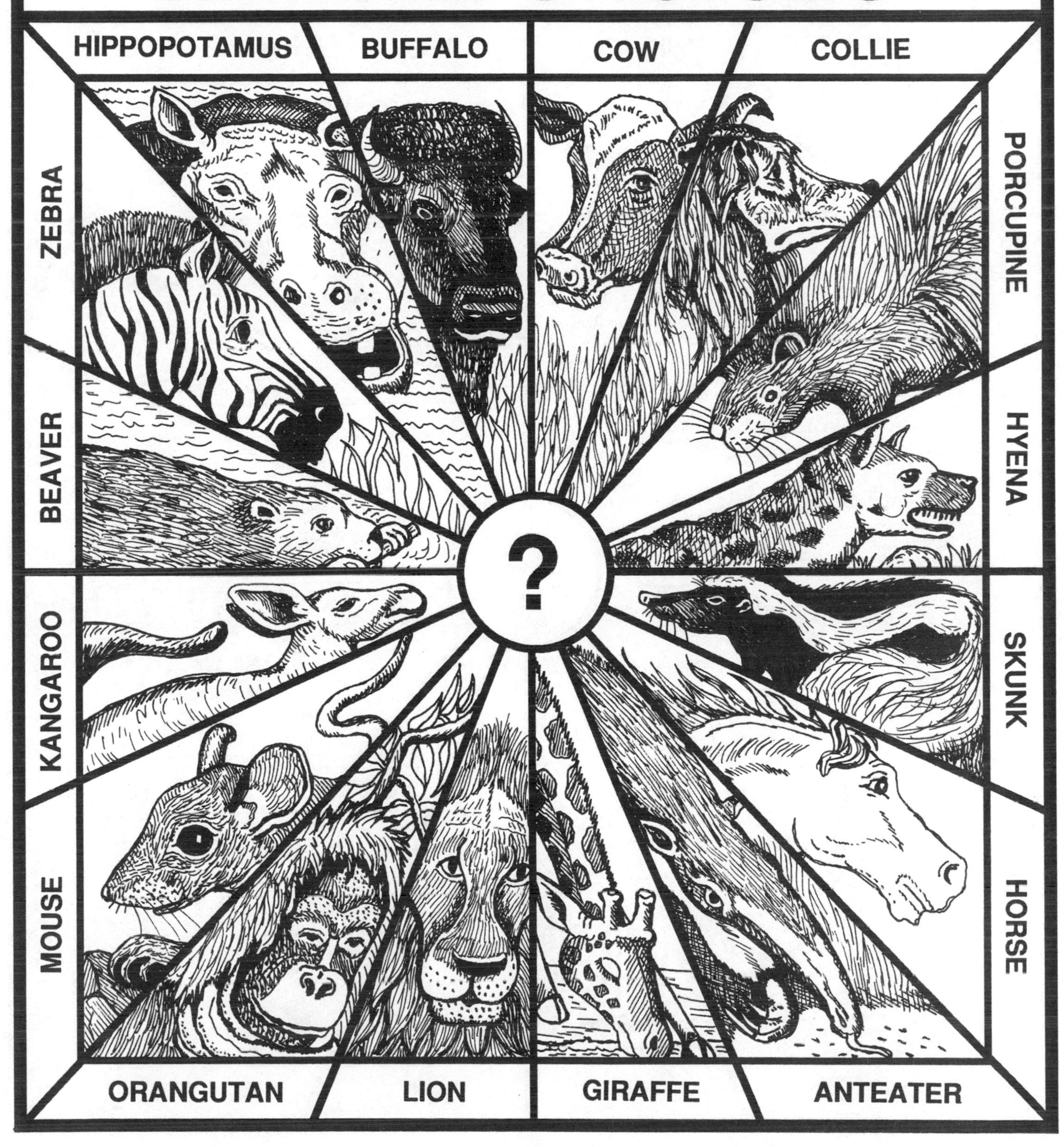

THE ADVENTURE

VEHICLE CHOICES

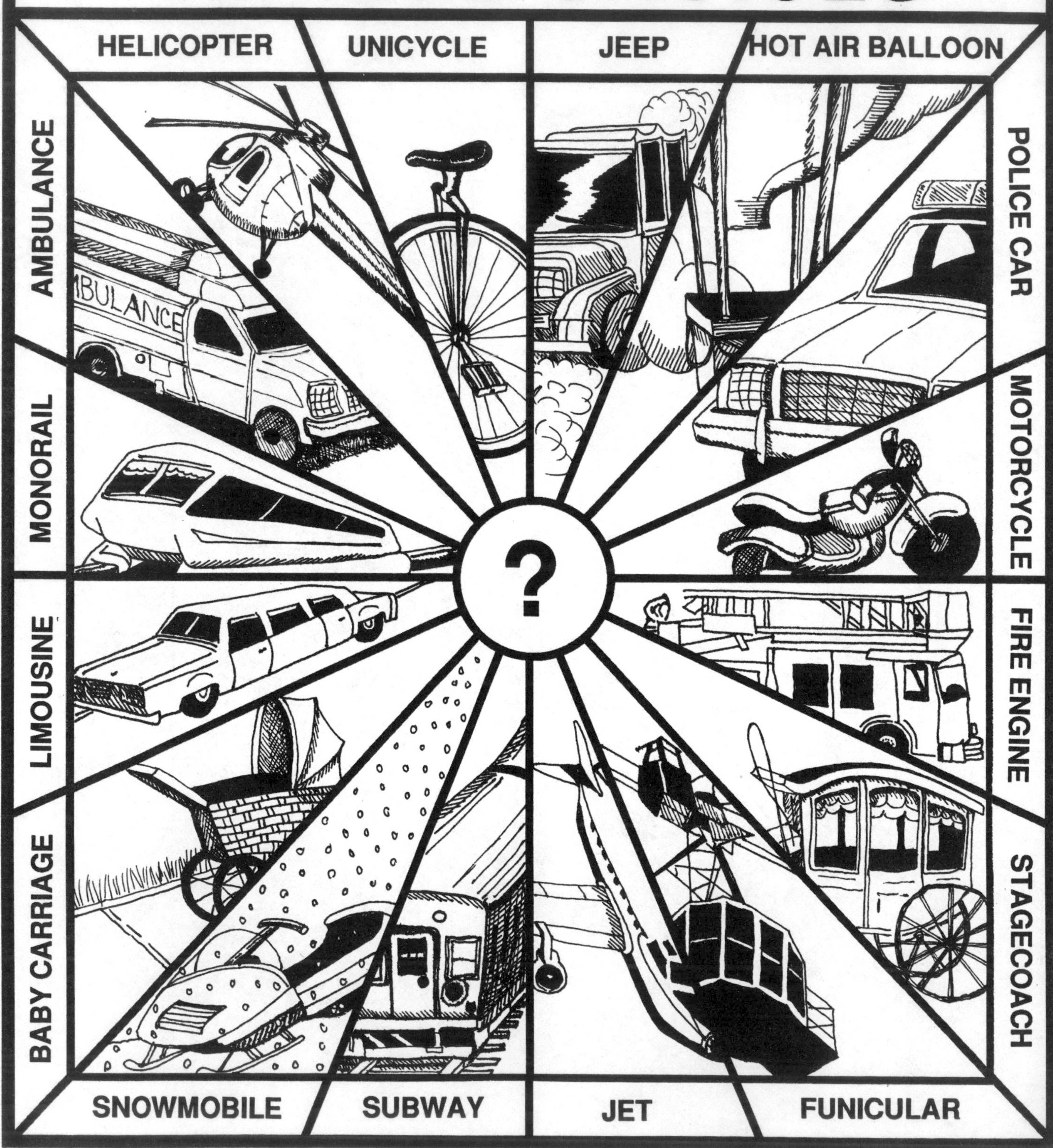

THE ADVENTURE

BIRD CHOICES

THE ADVENTURE

EQUIPMENT CHOICES

THE ADVENTURE

REPTILE CHOICES

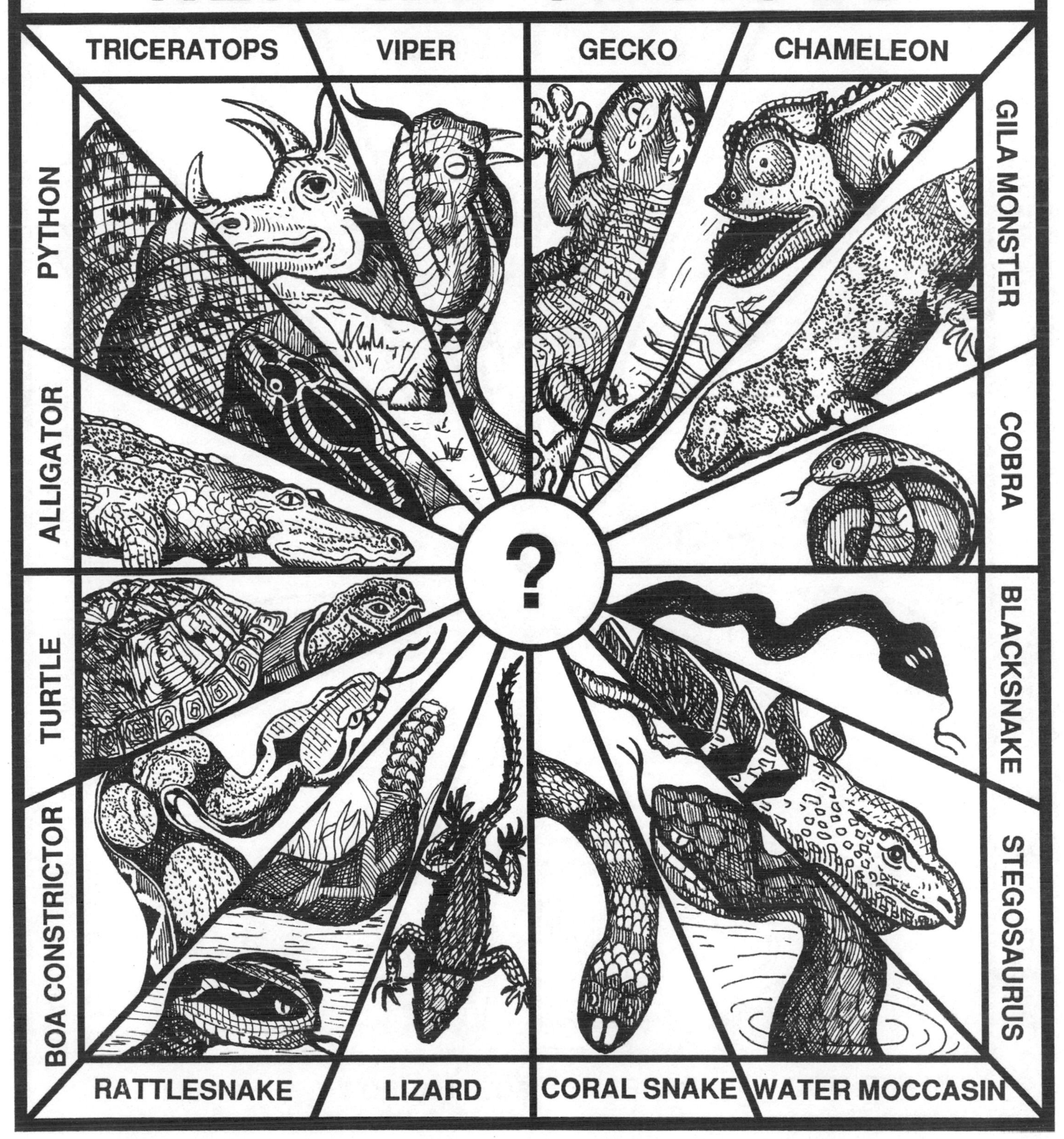

THE ADVENTURE

OBJECT CHOICES

THE ADVENTURE

INSECT CHOICES

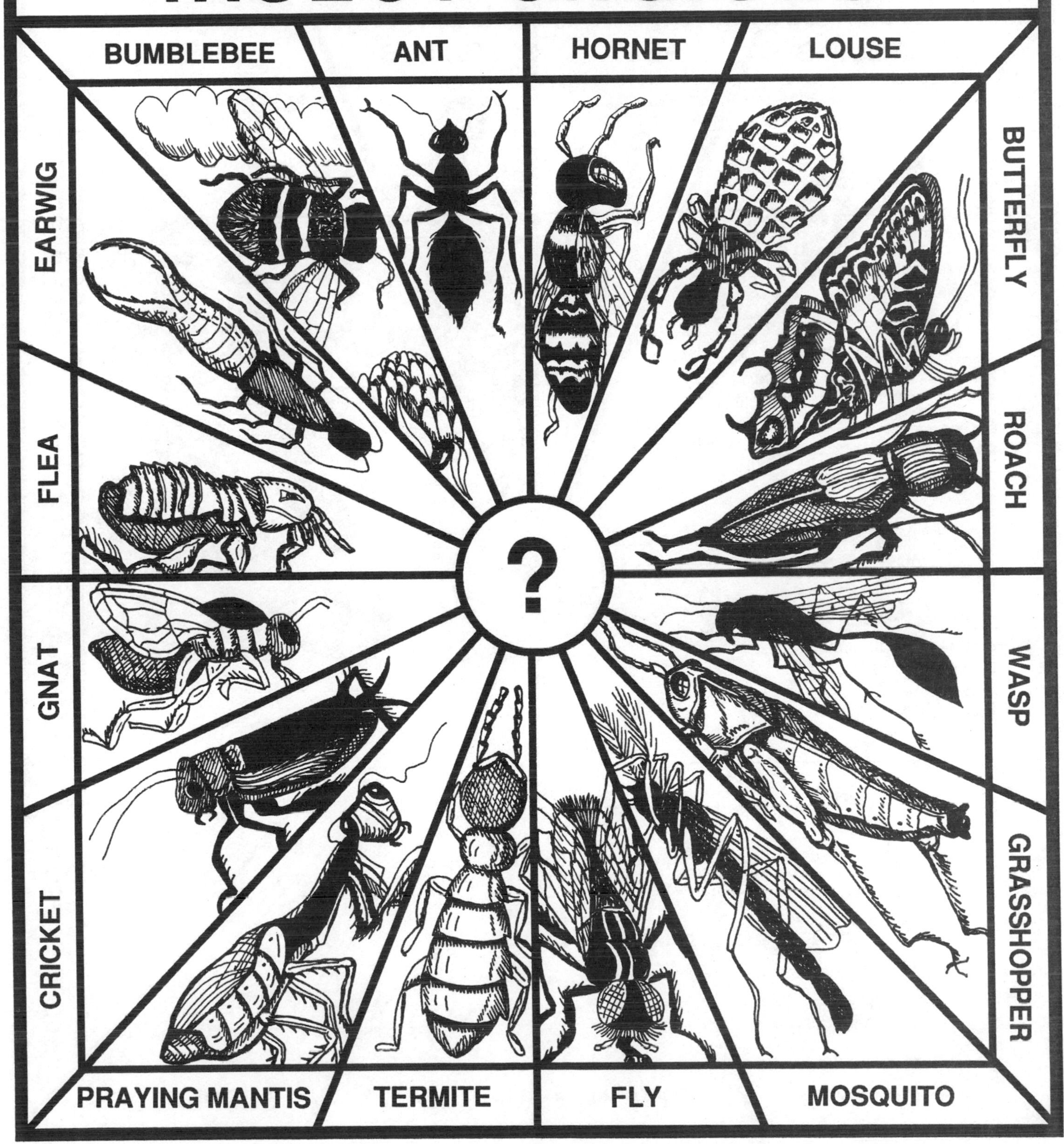

THE ADVENTURE

GARMENT CHOICES

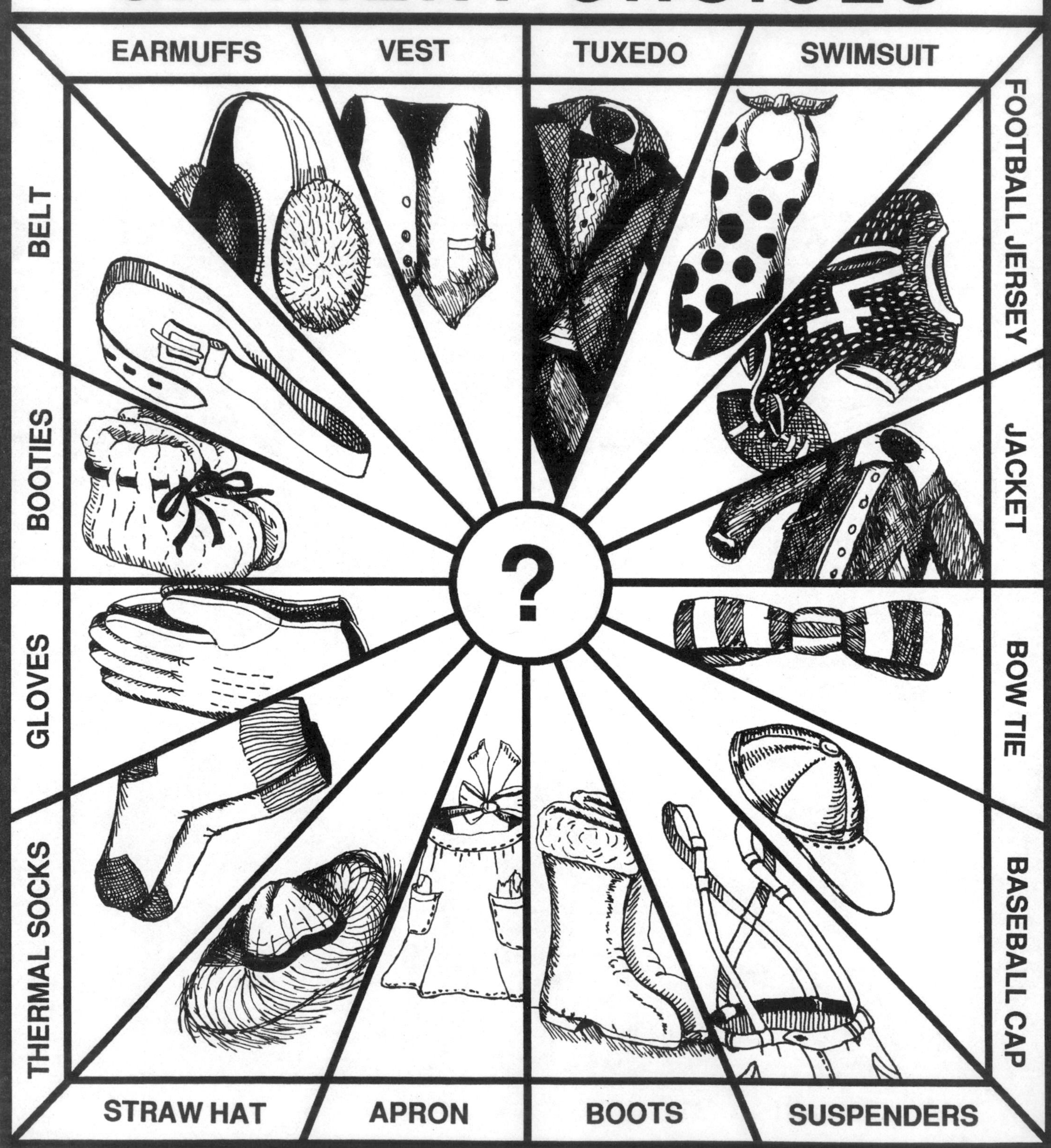

THE ADVENTURE

FOOD CHOICES

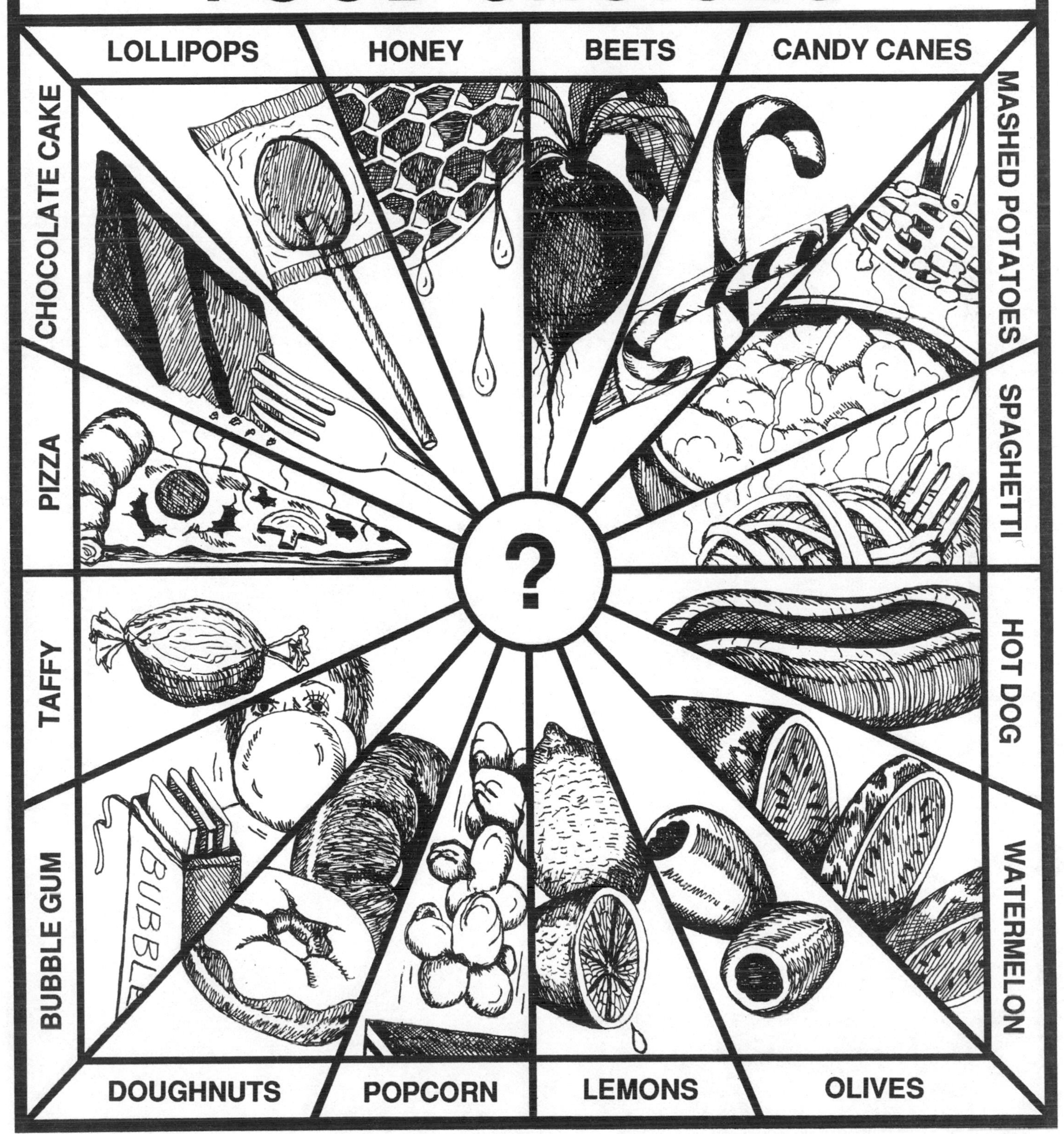

THE ADVENTURE

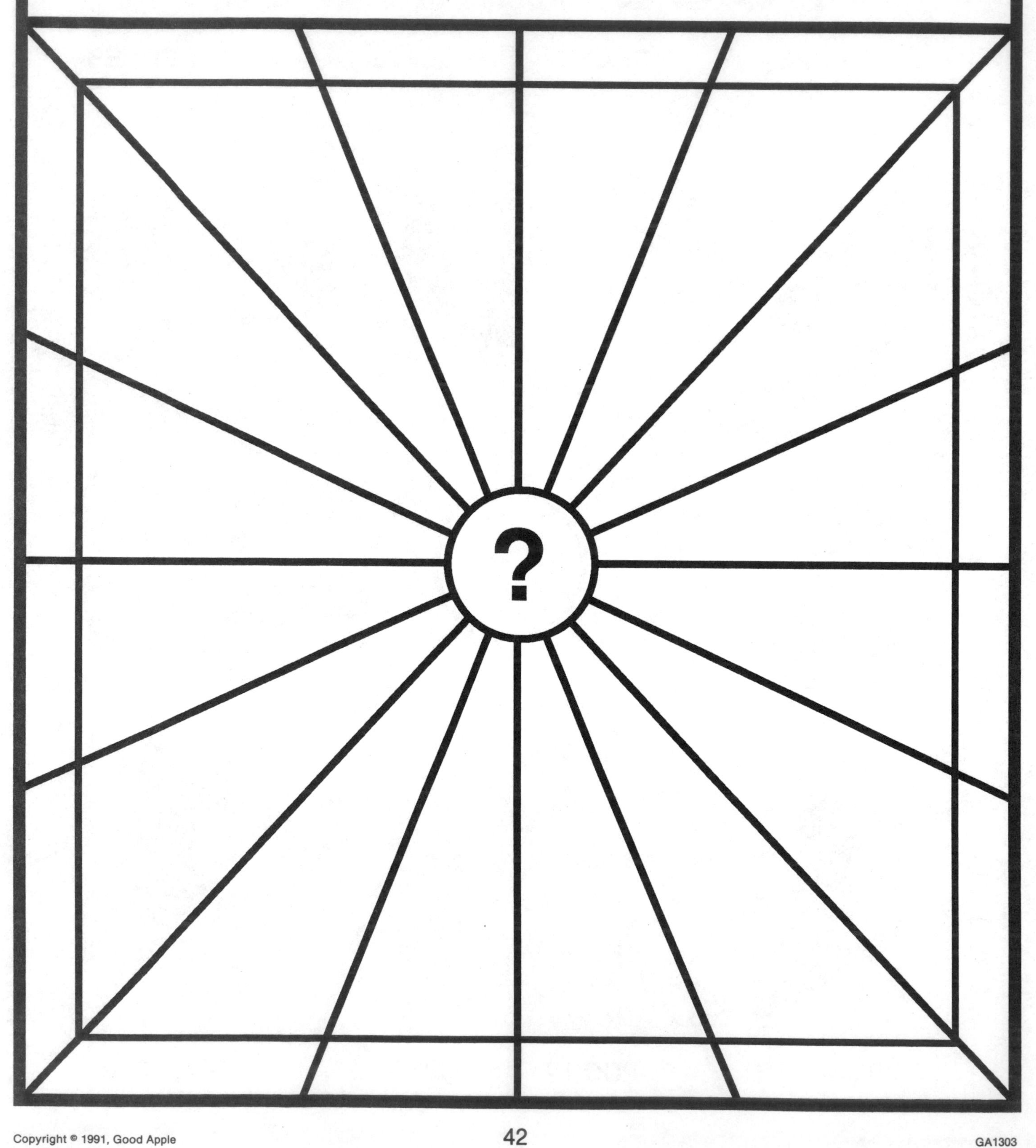

Cartoons for Creative Writing

Cartoons have universal appeal. Learners of practically all ages derive pleasure from reading and chuckling over them. Whenever possible, therefore, cartoons should be correlated with the development of academic skills.

The following ten pages contain cartoons which are designed to encourage students to write. These pages may be prepared for continued use in the classroom. Photocopy these pages onto heavy colorful paper or onto regular paper which may be mounted onto heavier paper. If desired, laminate or cover each page with clear self-adhesive paper. Cut into separate cards for a permanent writing activity.

The cartoon cards may be distributed in any desired manner for classroom, group, or individual writing activities. The techniques of writing models should be discussed prior to the use of this activity. Following the repeated part of each card are questions which may help the writer establish a model for the final product. All of the questions do not need to be answered in the writing assignment. All questions, however, should be **considered** prior to the *planning* of the writing task.

As an example, consider the first provided cartoon. The writing model (and example) for the planned response might be:

- Type of character
- Book being read
- Content of book
- What it made her do

One day a creature was wandering through a library. This creature was a spider! She was creeping through the children's book section, when suddenly she saw something she wanted to read. Yes, this spider was an unusual spider, because she could read very well!

The book she picked up was entitled ***Charlotte's Web****. Something about the book beckoned her. She was not sure why. However, when she opened it, she realized that it was a book about her great, great, great, great grandmother!*

Wow! She heard of the powerful deeds of this ancestor, and now she would be able to read about them herself! What a thrill she felt as she read first one chapter and then another. What fun it must have been to have saved a pig such as Wilbur!

Then she had an idea! There wasn't a pig on the grounds, but there ***was a turkey****. . . .*

An added blank page is provided which may be photocopied and used to prepare new cards for this activity. After the use of the provided cartoons, the teacher, parents, or students may search for additional cartoons which may be used for this exercise. Multitudes of these cartoons are available. Most daily newspapers have cartoons of interest to elementary age students. Weekly or monthly periodicals also have cartoons which appeal to this age. Individuals with artistic talents may also choose to draw cartoons for this activity. Following the collection of these items, several related questions should be carefully prepared which will challenge prospective writers. These questions may be written at the right of the cartoon.

Cartoons may be an unending source of academic enhancers. Clip them and use them!

Cartoons
for Creative Writing

Study the cartoon at the left. Write a short reaction to this cartoon. Before you write this reaction, think about the answers to the following questions: What type of character is shown in this cartoon? What book is this character reading? Will the content of the book be of any interest to this character? What might be an interesting outcome after the character has finished reading this book?

Cartoons
for Creative Writing

Study the cartoon at the left. Write a short reaction to this cartoon. Before you write this reaction, think about the answers to the following questions: What kind of character is shown in this cartoon? What might he have stolen? What could be happening inside his sack of stolen goods? What advice might you give him?

Cartoons
for Creative Writing

Study the cartoon at the left. Write a short reaction to this cartoon. Before you write this reaction, think about the answers to the following questions: What chore had the boy been asked to do? Did he finish it? Why not? What was his father's reaction? Was the boy's excuse a good one? What advice would you give him?

Cartoons
for Creative Writing

Study the cartoon at the left. Write a short reaction to this cartoon. Before you write this reaction, think about the answers to the following questions: What problem does the man have in this cartoon? What book is he trying to study in order to help with his problem? Do you remember that *The Jack Tales* is a collection of stories about a man named Jack? Is this the same kind of "jack" which this man is using? What advice would you give this man?

Cartoons
for Creative Writing

Study the cartoon at the left. Write a short reaction to this cartoon. Before you write this reaction, think about the answers to the following questions: Think about the term "car pool." Is it a *pool* where cars can go for a swim? Do cars swim? Tell what this term really means. Why could terms like this one be confusing to listeners or readers?

Cartoons
for Creative Writing

Study the cartoon at the left. Write a short reaction to this cartoon. Before you write this reaction, think about the answers to the following questions: What is the occupation of the man shown in this cartoon? To what organization does he belong? What kind of eating problem might he have? What does this problem have to do with the books he is holding? What advice would you give this man?

Cartoons
for Creative Writing

Study the cartoon at the left. Write a short reaction to this cartoon. Before you write this reaction, think about the answers to the following questions: What is the character shown in this cartoon? What problem might it be having? What is the topic of the book it is trying to read? Will this book help it with its problem? What advice would you give this character?

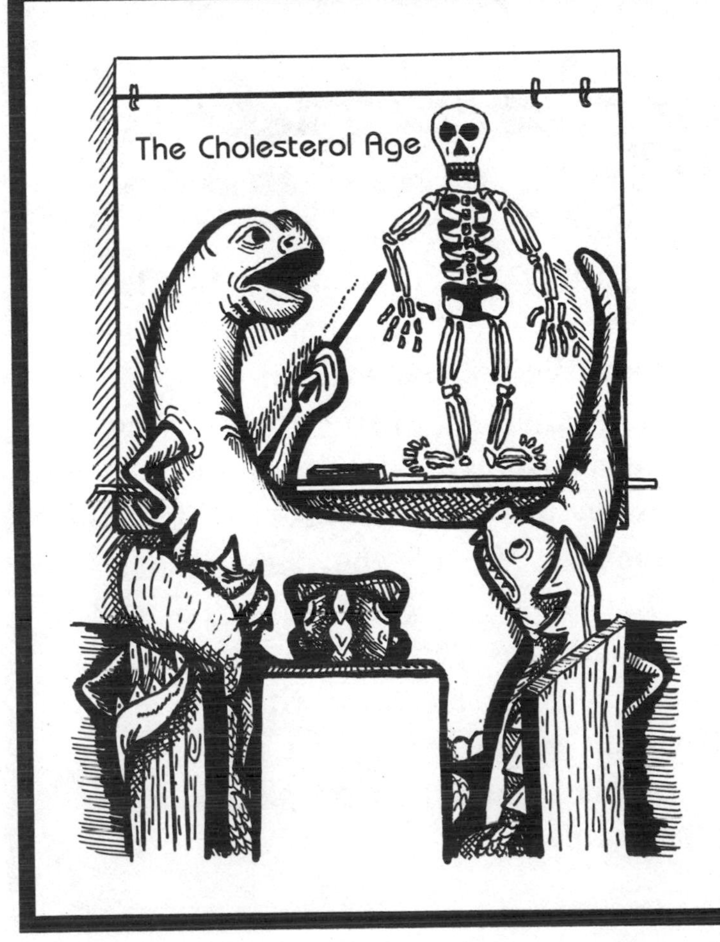

Cartoons
for Creative Writing

Study the cartoon at the left. Write a short reaction to this cartoon. Before you write this reaction, think about the answers to the following questions: When the dinosaurs roamed the earth, something happened to cause them to become extinct. Scientists have offered many reasons why this might have happened. If man had lived first and had become extinct, how might the dinosaurs have tried to explain the reasons? What is cholesterol? Can it cause mankind to become extinct?

Cartoons
for Creative Writing

Study the cartoon at the left. Write a short reaction to this cartoon. Before you write this reaction, think about the answers to the following questions: What has this waitress asked the diner? Why is the man puzzled? What do you think of the intelligence of this waitress? What advice would you give her?

Cartoons
for Creative Writing

Study the cartoon at the left. Write a short reaction to this cartoon. Before you write this reaction, think about the answers to the following questions: What are the differences in the two birdhouses in this cartoon? Would the term "snob" describe any of the birds shown? What conversation might the birds in the lower house have with the birds in the upper house? Do these birds remind you of any people you have known?

Cartoons
for Creative Writing

Study the cartoon at the left. Write a short reaction to this cartoon. Before you write this reaction, think about the answers to the following questions: What character is shown on the cover of this book? What is the book *The Velveteen Rabbit* about? If you were sharing the message of the book *The Velveteen Rabbit* with a friend, what might you say?

Cartoons
for Creative Writing

Study the cartoon at the left. Write a short reaction to this cartoon. Before you write this reaction, think about the answers to the following questions: What has the little boy in this picture given to his teacher? In what condition is it? How has this teacher reacted? What does the note say? What power can a small gift have on another, even if it is not expensive or in the best condition?

Cartoons
for Creative Writing

Study the cartoon at the left. Write a short reaction to this cartoon. Before you write this reaction, think about the answers to the following questions: What kind of problem is the animal in this cartoon trying to solve? Do you think it will work? Why do you think she has chosen this method of solving her problem? What advice would you give her?

Cartoons
for Creative Writing

Study the cartoon at the left. Write a short reaction to this cartoon. Before you write this reaction, think about the answers to the following questions: What character is shown in this cartoon? What feature of this character needs some improvement? What is the book this character is reading? How would you explain to this character the mistake it has made in selecting a book to read?

Cartoons
for Creative Writing

Study the cartoon at the left. Write a short reaction to this cartoon. Before you write this reaction, think about the answers to the following questions: What problem does the man in this cartoon have? What book is he reading? Do you think he will get any help from this book? What advice would you give this man?

Cartoons
for Creative Writing

Study the cartoon at the left. Write a short reaction to this cartoon. Before you write this reaction, think about the answers to the following questions: What is the meaning of the term "fan club"? When these two words are used separately they can have different meanings. What is another meaning of the word *fan?* What is another meaning of the word *club?* How has this store owner become confused with these words? What advice would you give him?

Cartoons
for Creative Writing

Study the cartoon at the left. Write a short reaction to this cartoon. Before you write this reaction, think about the answers to the following questions: What is unusual about the X ray which the doctor in this cartoon is showing his patient? How might he explain it to his patient? What might the patient's reaction be?

Cartoons
for Creative Writing

Study the cartoon at the left. Write a short reaction to this cartoon. Before you write this reaction, think about the answers to the following questions: Who is the man holding the book? Have you heard about or read the book *Curious George?* What is this book about? If the character shown in this picture really did read such a book, what might he be thinking?

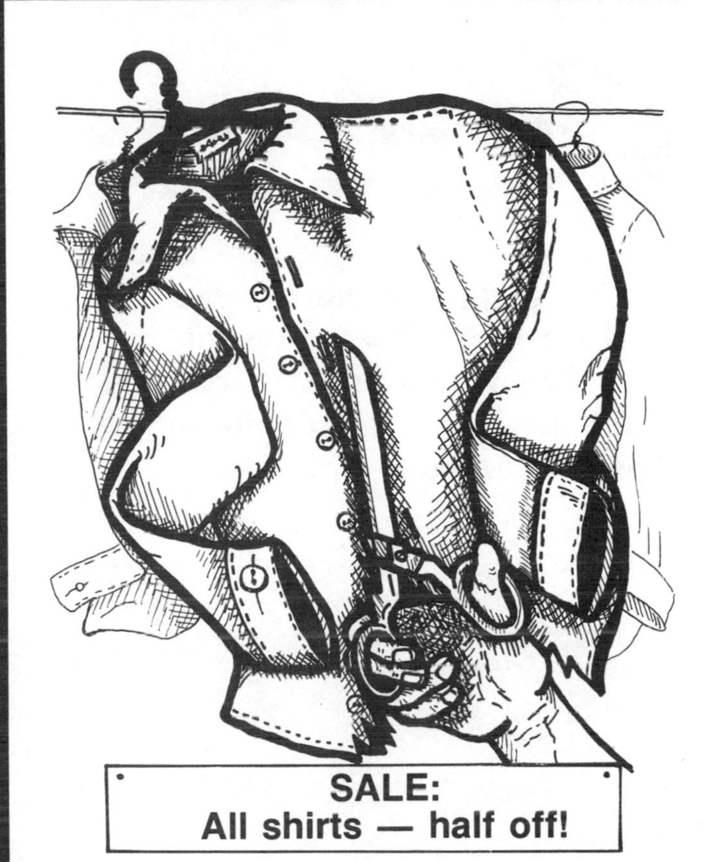

Cartoons
for Creative Writing

Study the cartoon at the left. Write a short reaction to this cartoon. Before you write this reaction, think about the answers to the following questions: What does the term "half off" mean when stores have sales? Does it mean that the garments are cut in half with scissors? Can this term be confusing to people who see the advertisements? Should these ads use other words instead? If you were a store owner, would you use these words?

Cartoons
for Creative Writing

Study the cartoon at the left. Write a short reaction to this cartoon. Before you write this reaction, think about the answers to the following questions: When some businesses have sales, the offer "two for the price of one" is frequently used. Was this a smart thing for a shoe store to offer? Why or why not? Will the customers be confused? What advice would you give the owner of this store?

Paste new cartoon here.

Cartoons
for Creative Writing

Study the cartoon at the left. Write a short reaction to this cartoon. Before you write this reaction, think about the answers to the following questions:

Paste new cartoon here.

Cartoons
for Creative Writing

Study the cartoon at the left. Write a short reaction to this cartoon. Before you write this reaction, think about the answers to the following questions:

FROM PICTURES TO WORDS

Pictures are invaluable tools for enhancing writing skills. Not only are they plentiful, but they can be very thought provoking for writers of any age.

The picture cards on the following pages are designed to aid in developing writing skills. These pages may be prepared for a reusable writing activity. Photocopy the sheets and mount onto heavy paper (or photocopy onto stiff colorful paper). If desired, laminate or cover each page with clear self-adhesive paper. Cut into separate picture cards for permanent writing materials.

These picture cards may be distributed in any desired manner for classroom, group, or individual writing activities. Writers should be encouraged to examine the picture very carefully and then read the provided story situation. On separate paper the writer then prepares a response to the situation described on the card.

A writing model should be first established for each written assignment. Implicit in each story starter are suggestions for such a model. Sample models may be demonstrated on the chalkboard before this task is pursued.

Future Picture Collections

A multitude of additional pictures may be gathered and prepared in a similar fashion for motivational writing materials. Such pictures appear in abundance in newspapers, catalogs, magazines, posters and books. When collected with care and organized in a thoughtful manner, these pictures may be used to motivate writers in the preparation of their future written materials. Many organizational systems exist for the gathering and filing of such pictures. One system is explained below.

Picture Groupings for Writing Experiences

When collecting pictures for writing experiences, be **selective.** Many teachers have begun with *one good* picture and have accomplished more than by having a larger quantity of less appealing pictures which were chosen haphazardly. Of course, attractive mounting will aid in the appeal. Start with some "choice" items and add only those which are especially eye-catching. After collecting several dozen, consider the following categories for their arrangement.

A. What Does This Person See?

These are pictures of individuals looking at something. The writer tells what he or she thinks the person sees. The wording of a samplc lead-in might be as follows: *Look at the person in this picture. He (She) is staring intently at something. What might it be?* This writing can begin at Step 1 in the Five-Step Writing Plan explained on page 6. Answers at the beginning of this experience might be similar to "A Ghost!" After several responses to these pictures, writers may gradually advance (with guidance via careful wording of leading questions) through each of the remaining steps in the Five-Step Writing Plan.

B. What Is This Person Saying?

These are pictures of individuals who are engaging in conversation. They may be used as suggested in Category A above. Writers may also advance through the Five-Step Writing Plan in a similar manner. If desired, the use of quotation marks may be taught with pictures in this category. (After choosing words which the person pictured might have said, these "spoken words" may be enclosed with quotation marks.)

C. What Is This Person's Problem?

These pictures are of individuals in some type of conflict. The writer may explain the problem and possible solutions.

D. Emotions

Pictures in this section are of individuals who are expressing some type of emotion. The writer is asked to identify the specific emotion portrayed (Step 1: Word) and explain the story behind it (Step 5: Story). The selected emotion may be used as the title of the story.

E. Group Interaction

These pictures may involve the same situations as explained in Categories A-D above, except that more than one person is shown.

F. Sports

These pictures include anything pertaining to sports. Various situations may be used such as the writer pretending he or she is a member of a team pictured. Topics such as sportsmanship may be included. Factual writing may include asking the writer to investigate rules, regulations, or facts of a pictured sport. Investigations of current sports heroes may also be a challenge.

G. Transportation

These pictures include a variety of different vehicles for transportation. A story starter may be used with a selected picture, such as the following example: *This is the only method of transportation which you have had during the past week. What was the most unusual thing that happened to you during that time?* If enough pictures are collected in this category, a separate one may be given to each writer. Other different experiences may be included, such as the following lead-in: *The cannibals have been chasing you through the forest for hours. You have run until your body almost refuses to obey. Suddenly you see the edge of the forest. About 100 yards (91 m) away are three vehicles of transportation. The cannibals are close behind you. You make a mad dash to get into one of the vehicles to try to escape. Unknown to you, only one of them contains gasoline. Tell what might happen.* (Sample pictures could be a tractor, an airplane, and a 1949 Chevrolet.)

H. Places to Live

These pictures may include some type of dwelling. They may be used in a similar manner as suggested in Category G.

I. Scenes

Pictures of beautiful or different scenes may be collected for this section. They may include any type of landscape or environmental setting. Use as suggested with Category G.

J. Animals

Animals generally have a very special appeal to young children. Pictures of them may be collected and used in many different types of writing activities.

K. Food

These pictures are of different types of food.

A multitude of them may be found in advertisements of monthly ladies' magazines. A variety of different writing experiences may result.

L. Anticipation

Pictures of a possible action may be gathered for this section. An example is a picture of a lion ready to pounce on an intended victim. The writer may prepare a story which predicts a possible outcome of the picture.

M. Career

These pictures show an adult performing a task involved in his or her chosen career. Many writing situations may occur with such pictures. Factual writing could include looking up facts about a chosen pictured career.

N. Fantasy

Fantasy pictures may include anything from comic book characters for younger writers or abstract designs for older learners. A story situation could be provided for each separate collected picture.

O. Holidays

Any holiday picture may be used for various writing experiences.

P. Mystery

A variety of pictures may be prepared for this category. Some pictures are mysterious as they are. Others may be modified by the cutting out and arranging of different objects (such as a knife, a clock, a key, or other "mystifying" items). The story to be written could include all pictured objects.

Q. What Is It?

This is related to the above category but it includes pictures of things which are not obvious. They may reflect an imaginary product which the writers will "sell" to the class members by writing an appropriate sales pitch for the "product." A sample lead-in for this task may be as follows: *"Zirgond" is a new product. You have been hired by the Zirgond Corporation to sell it from door to door. This picture shows how Zirgond looks. You give a sales pitch telling what it is, what it is used for, how it works, why the customer needs it, and how much it costs. You are now at your first door to sell it. Ding Dong!* (Note the implicit writing model in this story starter.)

R. Words

Sometimes large words or headlines may be cut out and mounted as a picture. These words could be used in a story or as titles or topics for stories. An example is a *Do Not Disturb* sign.

S. Miscellaneous

This category includes all motivating pictures which do not fit the above categories.

A variety of writing challenges may occur, depending upon the pictures collected. Often a story starter may be created with the use of pictures from several different categories. The following is an example: *You have been on a one-week vacation for two which you won when you entered the National Oatflakes Sweepstakes. This vacation was full of many surprises, and your story will reflect some of your adventures on this trip. This picture (selected from Categories A-D) shows the person who went with you on this vacation for two. This one (Category G) shows a vehicle of transportation which you used to travel to and from your vacation site and also during your vacation. This picture (Category H) shows the place you stayed during this vacation. This one (Category I) shows something you saw during this trip. This picture (Category J) shows an animal you encountered on this trip. This one (Category K) shows a food you had to eat each day you were away. (Others may be added as desired.) Tell a story about this vacation.*

The use of pictures is endless in the classroom. May they add pleasure and variety to the writing experience!

FROM PICTURES TO WORDS

The electricity has gone out in your home and you are holding a candle in order to see. Suddenly a strange noise comes from the next room. You must find out what it is. You are walking toward the door. Your body begins to shake. Tell what you will find in the next room.

FROM PICTURES TO WORDS

Your uncle has taken you fishing. You have been on the lake for hours but have not even had one nibble. Suddenly you feel a tug on your line. This is a big one! Perhaps it is as big as the one you heard your grandfather talk about years ago. You begin reeling in your line. Write the story you plan to tell about this catch after you return home.

FROM PICTURES TO WORDS

Your friends have dared you to explore Dead Man's Cave. They are so frightened of this cave that they refused to go close enough to watch you enter it. You don't believe their stories about what has happened to people and animals who have entered this cave. You are now crawling inside it. Tell what will happen.

FROM PICTURES TO WORDS

An elderly lady whom you know very well is walking up to your front door. You are the only person at home. She has a gift in her hands. Think about who the lady might be, why she has brought a gift, how long she might stay, and what she might say to you. Write a story about her gift and her visit.

FROM PICTURES TO WORDS

This has been the most eventful day of your life. Never did you believe that so much could happen in 24 hours! Your diary is in front of you. You are ready to write about the day's happenings. Tell what you plan to write.

FROM PICTURES TO WORDS

You and your family have taken a vacation to an exotic land. Early one morning you decide to take a walk on the beach. As the sun begins to rise, you suddenly notice a very strange and extremely large shell which perhaps washed up on the beach during the night. Describe the creature which might have come from this shell.

FROM PICTURES TO WORDS

You are sleeping soundly. Without warning you hear some creaks and groans coming from outside your window. A pair of scary eyes appear. When you awaken, how do you think you will react? How can such loud sounds and such a frightening set of eyes be explained?

FROM PICTURES TO WORDS

There is a new baby in your family. This baby is a surprise to everyone. Tell why this baby will now be in your family. Name it and tell some interesting things that will happen.

FROM PICTURES TO WORDS

Oh, no! You knew you should not have planted that strange seed! Just overnight a large stalk has appeared in your backyard. Something from the top seems to be calling you. You are deciding whether or not to climb the stalk and explore it. Tell what might happen.

FROM PICTURES TO WORDS

Your telephone is ringing. You are home alone. You have been expecting a call which is very important to you. Could this be it? Write a conversation which will include who the caller is, what the caller wants, and what your response will be.

FROM PICTURES TO WORDS

As you are driving down the highway, you notice a young boy sitting on his suitcase looking rather sad. You decide to find out if you can help him. Tell why he is on the side of the road, where he plans to go, and whether or not you will be able to help him.

FROM PICTURES TO WORDS

Your birthday present has just arrived. However, it is a dog. You did not want or ask for a dog. How will you treat the person who has given it to you? Tell what you will do with it.

FROM PICTURES TO WORDS

Your favorite friend has prepared a meal for you. This meal is in celebration of something special which has just occurred. The meal, however, is quite a surprise. Tell what the special event is and describe the meal.

FROM PICTURES TO WORDS

An admirer has brought a rose to you. This rose is being given to you for a very special reason. Tell who this admirer is, why the rose is being given to you, and whether or not you will accept it.

FROM PICTURES TO WORDS

You are a deep-sea diver. There have been reports about strange creatures that live underwater. You have been selected by the United States Deep-Sea Association to investigate these reports. You are now facing the problem. Describe what this problem is and explain in detail what you plan to do about it.

FROM PICTURES TO WORDS

You are helping your mother empty her shopping bags. Your hand is inside one of the bags. Suddenly you hear a voice coming from inside the bag. You realize that you are touching the thing that is making the noise. Write a conversation the two of you may have.

FROM PICTURES TO WORDS

You have opened a letter which reveals some very disturbing news. As you read it, you burst into tears. Tell what this news is, why it has happened, and what you plan to do about it.

FROM PICTURES TO WORDS

One spring morning you get up about an hour early. You look outside and see a dinosaur! Or do you? Are you dreaming? Did you step into a time machine in your sleep? Are your eyes deceiving you? Is someone playing a trick on you? Write a description of what might have happened.

FROM PICTURES TO WORDS

You have been chosen to be the next person to go up in space. You are now dressed and ready to enter the space shuttle. You have said good-bye to your family and friends. Write a story about the next several hours of your mission. Be sure to include why you are pursuing this mission.

FROM PICTURES TO WORDS

Cats cannot talk. However, your cat needs to tell you something. You pick it up to try to determine what is wrong. Look into its eyes. Tell what your cat's problem is and how you can help solve it.

BLANK EXPRESSIONS

The availability of adult party games such as ***Mad Libs*** and other companies' similar versions has offered an interesting concept for creating new classroom writing experiences.

Passages may be prepared which contain blank spaces to be completed with individual words, phrases, sentences, paragraphs, or longer selections. This activity can incorporate all steps in the Five-Step Writing Plan (explained on page 6).

The following pages provide examples which appeal to younger writers. They may write any desired response in the blank spaces provided. They may also use additional paper in cases when the space provided is not adequate to complete their stories.

To introduce this activity, one of the provided passages may be shown via an overhead projector. The viewers may discuss a variety of responses which could be used for the blank areas. Following this class discussion, the remaining individual sheets may be photocopied and used for additional writing experiences.

After the use of these provided pages, either the teacher or the students may prepare additional samples. Some interesting and unusual writing activities may occur as a result. Many existing writing materials may be used for these new passages. Consider the use of famous poems, proverbs, or other well-known works. An example might be ***The Night Before Christmas.*** The following is a suggested beginning:

'Twas the (1)_____ before (2)_______,
when all through the (3)___________
Not a (4)___________ was stirring,
not even a (5)__________;
The (6)__________ were hung
by the (7)__________ with care
In hopes that (8)__________
soon would be there.

The above passage could be continued with significant nouns, adjectives, or verbs omitted.

For passages such as the above, a separate sheet of items could be prepared which would respond to the sample containing blanks. This sheet could be given to the writers ***without*** their knowing what the items would be matching. The following is the start of such a list:

1. Name a time of day. __________
2. Name a holiday. __________
3. Name a building. __________
4. Name an animal. __________
5. Name a different animal. __________
6. Name a garment. (Plural) __________
7. Name a part of a house. __________
8. Name someone everyone in this class knows. __________

After writers have filled in the blank spaces in a sample such as the above, they would then be given the copy of the **original passage** for a *transfer* of their written choices. (Remember that writers should **not be informed** of the association with ***The Night Before Christmas*** as they are making their selections.) Both portions of the above may be continued for a complete writing activity at Christmas. Hilarious scripts frequently result.

An abundance of additional passages may be considered for this exercise. Shakespearian sonnets, the melodies to currently popular songs, jump rope jingles, and other such material may be prepared. Learners may create their own passages for others to complete. Such possibilities are endless.

The Unusual Breakfast Cereal

(Write one or more words in each blank space.)

As I was helping my mom shop for food, I saw a new cereal on the shelf. I picked up the ________________ box and was surprised to see ________________ on the ____________. It looked ________________, so I ______________________________. Then my mom yelled, "______________________________!"

But before I could ________________________

____

____

____

____

____

____

____

____

____

____

____

____

(Use more paper if you wish.)

The Car I Want

(Write one or more words in each blank space.)

The car I plan to buy will be very different from all others. It will have ______________ where most ______________ are. It will not ______________ ______________ unless it ______________!

Most people will think it ______________________________
____

But that won't bother me because ______________
____
____
____
____
____
____
____
____
____
____
____

(Use more paper if you wish.)

My Birthday Surprise

(Write one or more words in each blank space.)

On the evening of my ______________ birthday, I heard the sound of ______________________ in the ______________. It was hard to ______________ because of the ______________ so I ____________.

All at once ____

____

____

____

____

____

____

____

____

____

____

____

____

(Use more paper if you wish.)

The Strange Wedding

(Write one or more words in each blank space.)

Yesterday I went to a ________________ wedding. The ______________ bride was ________________ as she ____________________. Only once did the groom ever ______________ the ______________ until he ______________________. Everyone then suddenly ____________________ to the ________________ while ______________________________.

Strangest of all was ___________________________

____

____

____

____

____

____

____

____

____

____

____

(Use more paper if you wish.)

The Talking Frog

(Write one or more words in each blank space.)

Everyone knows that frogs do not talk. However, yesterday as I was ______________ in my backyard, I suddenly heard a ____________ noise. I looked up and saw a ______________________________ frog.

"____!"

the frog yelled.

"____,"

I answered.

"____,"

was its reply.

____

____

____

____

____

____

____

____

____

(Use more paper if you wish.)

My New Neighbor

(Write one or more words in each blank space.)

Late last month a new family moved into the empty house across the street. How surprised I was when I first met Ronald! His ________________ were as ________________ as ______________. And even his ______________ were ________________.

Never before have I ever seen a ________________ on someone's ________________________________.
He had ________________ over his ________________ and ________________ covering his ______________.
My family laughed when he ________________ over the ________________________________.

But before long he ____________________________

____

____

____

____

____

____

____

(Use more paper if you wish.)

The Angry Insect

(Write one or more words in each blank space.)

As I was on my way to school very early this morning, a ______________________________ flew past my ______________________________. I could tell it was ______________________________ because its ________________ were ________________ ______________________________.

Suddenly I felt ______________________________.

Then to my surprise ______________________________

____

____

____

____

____

____

____

____

____

____

(Use more paper if you wish.)

How to Look Smart

(Write one or more words in each blank space.)

A new product is now for sale which can make anyone look smart. It is called ________________. A man from ________________ has just discovered that a ________________ of ________________ will make ________________________________!

You must use it ________________________________

____

But it will work only if you ________________

____

____

____

____

____

____

____

____

____

____

(Use more paper if you wish.)

Our Family Vacation

(Write one or more words in each blank space.)

Last ______________ my family decided to go on a ______________ vacation to the ____________.

Early one morning we all got up and quickly put on our ____________________________. We drove to the ____________________________. There we saw ______________________________ covered with ______________________________ from ______________ to ____________.

We saw large ____________ which looked as if they were ______________________________.

When my mom asked if I wanted to go back to the same place next year, I told her ____________________
____
____
____
____
____
____

(Use more paper if you wish.)

My Doctor's Advice

(Write one or more words in each blank space.)

One day last week my doctor gave me some very ______________ advice. He told me that I should never ________________ again and that I should stop ____________________. He also said that my ____________ was ____________ and that my ______________ might stop _____________ if I didn't ___________.

Then he told me to take _______________ for my ____________.

But when he told me that my ____________ was ____________, I almost ____________!

As I left, ______________________________

____

____

____

____

____

____

____

(Use more paper if you wish.)

★ ★ THE NEIGHBORHOOD NEWS ★ ★

Many writing activities involve the use of various *creative* experiences. **The Neighborhood News** begins with printed material which is based on **facts** and proceeds through both factual and creative writing experiences.

The following pages contain reports of **true** events which have been described in various local and national newspapers. These incidents have been **rewritten** for many reasons. In most cases the real names of the individuals have been changed. The locations of most events have either been omitted or changed. However, the story content in each case is based upon ***a true happening.***

Students should be instructed to read these news articles (which may be photocopied and prepared in a reusable manner). Following each article is a description of a writing assignment. On separate paper the learners prepare their responses.

A discussion of both the Five-Step Writing Plan (explained on page 6) may be incorporated with this task. One news article may be selected for the purpose of discussing each step. An example might be the one entitled "Home Sweet Home." For Step 1, ask learners to provide other words which have more than one meaning. These may be listed on the chalkboard as they are volunteered. For Step 2, ask learners for one meaning of the word **home.** Phrases such as *a dwelling place, a place for people with special needs,* or *a rubber slab at one corner of a baseball diamond* may be offered. This type of experience may gradually advance to the final step.

Writing models may also be discussed. Although each news article would have its own set of possibilities, generic models may be discussed. This discussion may begin with one of the provided articles. A model for the one mentioned in the above paragraph might be as follows: *Identification of the problem word, an explanation of a possible funny situation which may occur (from one to five paragraphs), and a summary or conclusion as the final paragraph.*

A final blank page is offered for the preparation of additional interesting news articles. Either students or teachers may search for true reported happenings which form the basis for future writing experiences. Because people are "human," they will supply future writers with a multitude of experiences for stories. These articles, however, may need to be edited for various reasons before being pasted onto the photocopied blank pages. Be careful not to clip articles which would be an embarrassment to any class member. A writing lead-in should be prepared for each one.

★ ★ THE NEIGHBORHOOD NEWS ★ ★

Volume 1 .... A SPECIAL EDITION .... 50 cents

Baby Falls Three Floors

Don Steed was walking by Moore Apartments when he heard a strange sound. He looked up and saw an eleven-month-old baby sitting under the railing of a balcony three floors up. The baby looked down and lost her balance. Within seconds she toppled off the edge.

Steed raced toward the falling child who barely landed in his arms. The mother was inside talking on the telephone. She was not aware that her child was on the balcony. Except for being scared, both Steed and the baby are doing fine.

Writing Fun: *Steed has decided to give a talk at the local "Mom's Club" about child safety. Tell how he might relate this event to his talk with them.*

★ ★ THE NEIGHBORHOOD NEWS ★ ★

Volume 2 .... A SPECIAL EDITION .... 50 cents

Woman Lives with Rats

Neighbors of a Miami woman reported seeing dozens of rats through her windows as they walked by her house. When the police were called, an officer went to her home.

"You have rats in your house," the officer told her after he saw about thirty of them running across the floor.

"I know it. It's none of your business. I'm not breaking any law!" the woman said as she slammed the door in his face. Further police investigation revealed that there really was no law against having rats in one's home.

Writing Fun: *Write a conversation this woman might have had with her rats after the officer left.*

★ ★ THE NEIGHBORHOOD NEWS ★ ★

Volume 1 . . . . A SPECIAL EDITION . . . . 50 cents

Foot-in-Mouth Disease?

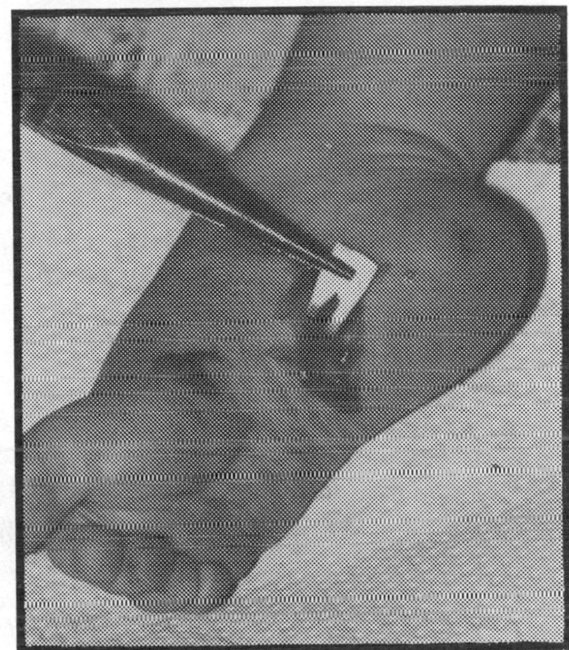

Tim Richmond began having problems as he walked. Soon he was unable to stand up without much pain in his foot.

His parents took him to their doctor who soon discovered the problem. Tim had a tooth growing in his foot!

Writing Fun: *Sometimes strange things do actually happen to the human body. Also we sometimes hear stories which have not really happened at all, but which are told as a truth. Write such a story. Make sure this story relates to the human body.*

★ ★ THE NEIGHBORHOOD NEWS ★ ★

Volume 2 . . . . A SPECIAL EDITION . . . . 50 cents

Sneezing Problems

Doctors were puzzled after Jan French sneezed for eighty-three days. Dr. Mel Howe at first thought she might be suffering from allergies. Ms. French had reported having a bad cold and sniffles. Those sniffles turned into spells of sneezing which have lasted as long as six hours. At times the sneezes were only thirty seconds apart. Ms. French says she can't sleep well or go to work. Three times she blew out parts of her metal braces as she sneezed. Two of the area doctors are now studying the problem. They hope to find a solution soon.

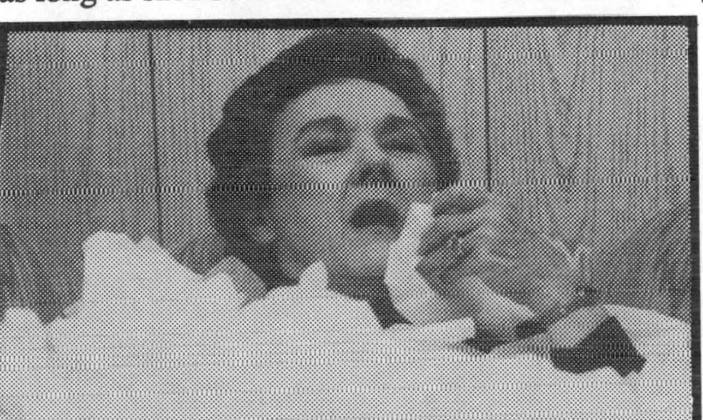

Writing Fun: *Many remedies for sneezing have been offered. Think of a very different solution to offer Ms. French to help solve her problem of sneezing.*

★ ★ THE NEIGHBORHOOD NEWS ★ ★

Volume 1 .... A SPECIAL EDITION .... 50 cents

Potato Chip Surprise

Sally Jenkins found quite a surprise when she opened a large bag of potato chips for the family picnic. Her hand felt something strange, quite unlike potato chips. It was a man's wallet. Money, driver's license, credit cards, and eight pictures were inside. Ms. Jenkins located the owner of the wallet through the address on his driver's license. The man worked at Pop's Potato Chip Factory. He was greatly relieved to have his wallet returned to him.

Writing Fun: *It is rare that any object can accidentally get inside a packaged bag of chips. However, it is possible. Write another story which tells about a different object that could fall into a bag of chips.*

★ ★ THE NEIGHBORHOOD NEWS ★ ★

Volume 2 .... A SPECIAL EDITION .... 50 cents

The Money Lunch

The three sons of Bill Walters may be $7000 richer. They were playing at the edge of Blue Forest Playground last month when they found a small bag of 20-dollar bills. They thought it was someone's discarded lunch bag. They gave it to their father who turned it over to the police. So far no one has claimed it. It will later belong to the three sons if the owner is not found.

Writing Fun: *If you found a bag containing $7000, tell what you would do with it. (Would you keep it, give it to your parents, turn it over to the police, or do something different?)*

★ ★ **THE NEIGHBORHOOD NEWS** 

Volume 1 . . . . A SPECIAL EDITION . . . . 50 cents

Woman Plans to Marry Cannibal

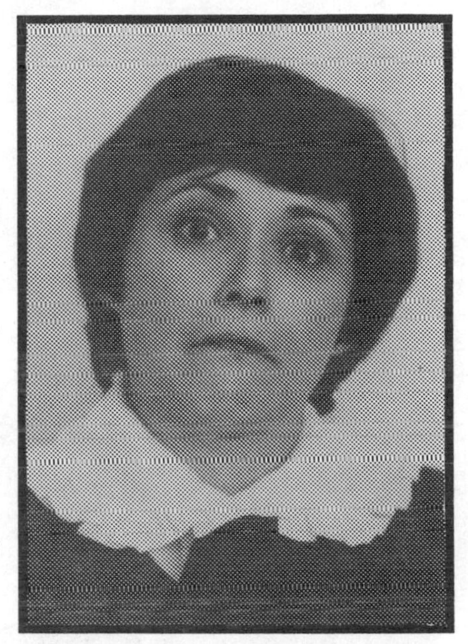

The wedding of Miss Linda Wells will be held Friday of next week. She plans to marry a cannibal from Africa. (Cannibals are people who eat human flesh. The practice exists today only in Africa, Asia, and the Pacific Islands.)

Miss Wells told reporters that she will not be living in the United States after her wedding.

No mention was made regarding thc wedding feast.

Writing Fun: *Write a description of a meal this couple might plan to serve the wedding guests.*

★ ★ **THE NEIGHBORHOOD NEWS** ★ ★

Volume 2 . . . . A SPECIAL EDITION . . . . 50 cents

Sister Is "Rattled"

The parents of Tim and Jenny Mason gave clear instructions about the appearance and sound of the poisonous rattlesnake before the family went on a camping trip.

After walking a few yards from the family tent, Jenny heard the sound of the deadly rattlesnake. She screamed for her parents. A quick search revealed brother Tim in the bushes shaking a glass bottle half filled with vitamin pills.

Tim was punished for his prank.

Writing Fun: *Describe the punishment you feel would be appropriate for Tim in this case.*

★ ★ THE NEIGHBORHOOD NEWS ★ ★

Volume 1 . . . . A SPECIAL EDITION . . . . 50 cents

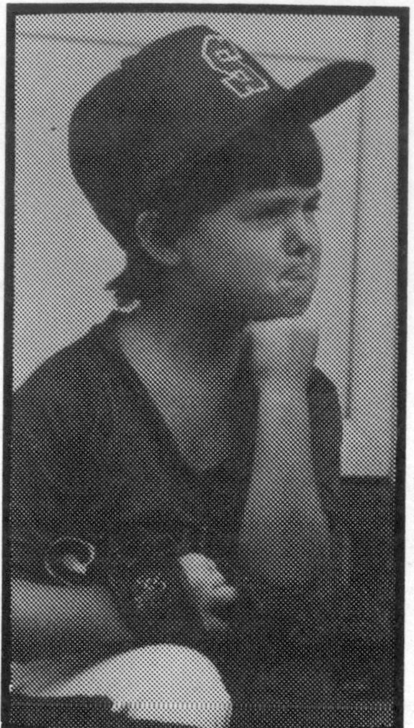

Home Sweet Home

The Big Lake Church baseball team had only eight players for their last game. The coach saw five-year-old Jerry Cole who lived across the street and asked him to play.

"Just do **exactly** as I tell you to do," the coach told Jerry when it was his turn at bat. The coach then asked him not to swing at the ball in hopes the pitcher would walk him. That did happen. The next batter hit a triple and ran for first base. But Jerry did not know what to do.

"Go home, Jerry!" yelled the coach. And that is just what Jerry did. He ran from first base to his own front door of his "home."

Writing Fun: *Jerry became confused because of the two meanings of the word* ***home.*** *Think of another word which has more than one meaning. Write a funny story about that word.*

★ ★ THE NEIGHBORHOOD NEWS ★ ★

Volume 2 . . . . A SPECIAL EDITION . . . . 50 cents

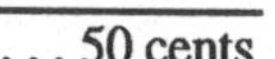

Cat Shoots Owner

A cat named Tabby shot his owner last week. Gary Davis, the cat's owner, was admitted to the City Hospital for a gunshot wound in his left arm.

Davis said he was cleaning his guns and left them on the dining room table when he turned to get a drink. As Tabby jumped from the top of the refrigerator, her paw struck the trigger of one of the loaded guns.

When the police checked out the story, they found several paw prints on the top of the refrigerator.

Writing Fun: *If cats could talk, write what you think this cat might have said after the shooting.*

★ ★ THE NEIGHBORHOOD NEWS ★ ★

Volume 1 . . . . A SPECIAL EDITION . . . . 50 cents

The Ten-Foot Cookie

The owners of Chip's Cookie Company advertised their cookies in a different way. They used a special oven in the mall parking lot to make one big chocolate chip cookie which was ten feet (3.04 m) in length. The radio stations announced that anyone who came by could eat part of this cookie. By the end of the day over 2500 people had tasted it.

Writing Fun: *If someone gave you a ten-foot cookie, tell what you might do with it.*

★ ★ THE NEIGHBORHOOD NEWS ★ ★

Volume 2 . . . . A SPECIAL EDITION . . . . 50 cents

World's Biggest Eater

Bozo Miller of California is the world's biggest eater. Without stopping, he has eaten 75 roast beef sandwiches, 324 ravioli, 27 two-pound (.90 kg) chickens, and 30 servings of chocolate pudding.

Miller is five-foot-seven (1.70 m) and weighs 285 pounds (128.25 kg). His waist measures 57 inches (1.42 m). Each day he consumes 25,000 calories. That is about twelve times the amount of food eaten by the average man.

★ ★ THE NEIGHBORHOOD NEWS ★ ★

Volume 1 . . . . A SPECIAL EDITION . . . . 50 cents

Dinosaur Eggs?

Workers at the Plain Digging Company last week dug up what they thought were dinosaur eggs.

Two men uncovered about twenty round, heavy objects. After careful washings, however, the men decided that they were old bowling balls.

People in the town remembered that a bowling alley had been on the construction site. It had burned a few years earlier.

Writing Fun: *Describe one use for twenty old bowling balls.*

★ ★ THE NEIGHBORHOOD NEWS ★ ★

Volume 2 . . . . A SPECIAL EDITION . . . . 50 cents

Joyride for Infant

A four-month-old baby took an interesting ride last Saturday. She and her parents, Mr. and Mrs. Bill Moss, were returning from their trip to a nearby city. Their car had become messy and untidy. Mr. Moss pulled into a parking lot and both parents began to clean out the car. They placed the baby girl in her car seat and put both on top of the car while they cleaned up. After the car was neat again, the couple pulled out of the parking lot—*with the baby still on top of the car*. Another driver noticed what had occurred and gradually stopped them. There was no serious injury to the child.

Writing Fun: *If this four-month-old baby could talk, what do you think she would be saying as she was riding on the top of the car?*

★ ★ THE NEIGHBORHOOD NEWS ★ ★

Volume 1 .... A SPECIAL EDITION .... 50 cents

Man Lives in Cardboard Box

Larry Stark told New York reporters that he has lived in a cardboard box for three years. Stark said that when he ran out of money, he had no place to go. Therefore, he found a box in which a refrigerator had been shipped, and he turned it into his home. Stark had no known relatives.

"Things could be worse," Stark said when asked about his home. He had suffered through three cold winters in his box.

Writing Fun: *If you were going to live in a box for three years, describe in detail the kind of box you hope it would be.*

★ ★ THE NEIGHBORHOOD NEWS ★ ★

Volume 2 .... A SPECIAL EDITION .... 50 cents

Burglar Stuck in Chimney

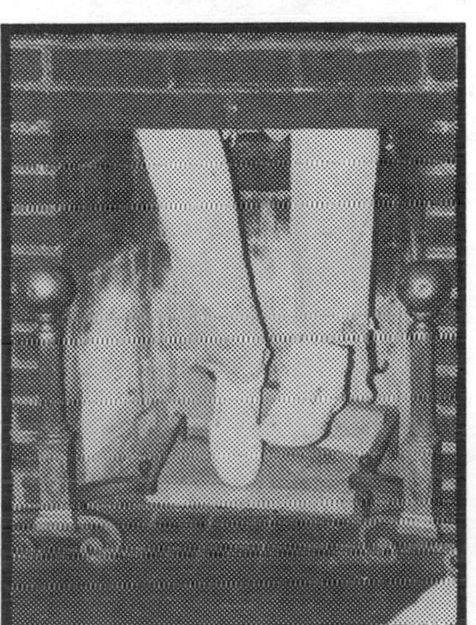

Rick Laws decided to rob the home of a nearby elderly couple while they were away. Some neighbors, however, saw Laws enter the house and they called the police.

When Laws heard the siren, he looked for a place to hide. The closest place was the chimney. Laws pulled himself up far enough to hide his body. However, he was soon stuck. His only hope was to let the police know that he was trapped in the chimney.

Laws not only had to serve time in jail, but he had to stay in the hospital also. Laws developed lung problems soon after his encounter in the much-used fireplace.

Writing Fun: *Describe the lesson Laws might have learned from his experience in the chimney.*

★ ★ THE NEIGHBORHOOD NEWS ★ ★

Volume 1 . . . . A SPECIAL EDITION . . . . 50 cents

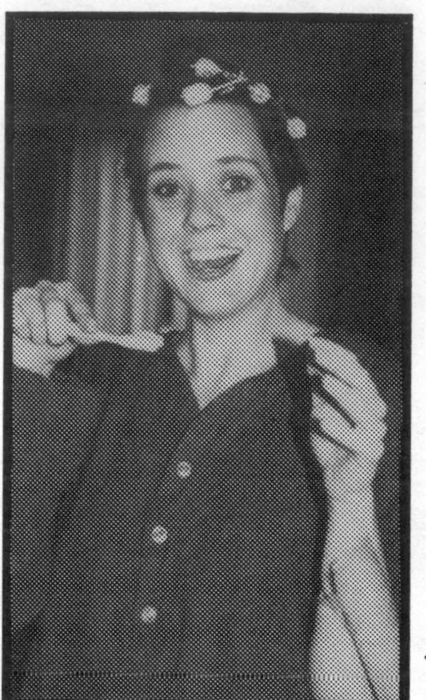

A Bad Scene

Friday night was to be Connie's first date with her high school's star football player. However, he arrived early—and left early.

When he rang Connie's doorbell, she thought it might be another friend. She answered—with rollers in her hair, toothbrush in her hand, *and an ear of frozen corn tied to her arm.*

Earlier Connie had fallen on her arm. To keep it from swelling, she decided to use an ice pack. Having no ice and running out of time, she used the first thing she found that was cold: a frozen ear of corn. For Connie, it was a bad scene. Her friends now call her "Corny Connie."

Writing Fun: *Think of a nickname you have heard used for one of your friends. Tell a story about how this friend might have acquired this nickname.*

★ ★ THE NEIGHBORHOOD NEWS ★ ★

Volume 2 . . . . A SPECIAL EDITION . . . . 50 cents

Skunks Present Problems

Four skunks have made their home underneath the back porch of the Mathes home.

Todd Mathes called the city dogcatcher who informed Mathes that he could not help with his skunk problem. Mathes then called the city council, the Health Department, and the local Animal Care Unit.

"I even asked for help from radio and television stations," he complained.

It seems that Mathes is "stuck" with his skunks for now.

Writing Fun: *You have a solution to help the Mathes family get rid of their skunks! Describe your plan.*

★ ★ THE NEIGHBORHOOD NEWS ★ ★

Volume 1 . . . . A SPECIAL EDITION . . . . 50 cents

Husband for Sale?

Mrs. Joyce Smith claimed that her husband did not pay enough attention to her. She also accused him of not helping her with the tasks at home. She decided to place an ad in the newspaper to see if he would notice.

The ad read *"Husband for Sale or Trade! Will trade for any of the following items: washing machine, clothes dryer, vacuum cleaner, or television set. Product must be in better shape than husband."*

She reported that within three days she received almost a hundred calls.

***Writing Fun:** Write a conversation Ms. Smith might have had with someone who called about this ad.*

★ ★ THE NEIGHBORHOOD NEWS ★ ★

Volume 2 . . . . A SPECIAL EDITION . . . . 50 cents

Turkey Jogger?

Jack Boyd has a very different pet with a strange habit. It jogs.

Each morning as Boyd jogs through the neighborhood, his pet turkey follows behind him. The turkey always runs at the same speed as Boyd.

Boyd stated that no matter how fast he ran, his turkey always stayed about two yards away. So far, no one has bothered the turkey.

***Writing Fun:** Pretend that Boyd has found a new hobby and his turkey wants to be a part of it with him. Name the hobby and write a funny scene which might occur.*

★ ★ THE NEIGHBORHOOD NEWS ★ ★

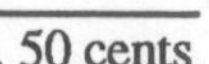

Volume 1 . . . . A SPECIAL EDITION . . . . 50 cents

The Blacksnake

Mrs. Pam Oaks locked herself inside her outdoor shed last Friday until her husband came home from work. As she heard the family car pull into the driveway, she screamed for her husband to "kill the snake, then open the shed." Her husband laughed as he lifted the black garden hose which he had earlier tossed into the weeds near the shed. Ms. Oaks failed to see what was so funny.

Writing Fun: *Compare a blacksnake with a black garden hose by telling five ways they are either alike or different.*

★ ★ THE NEIGHBORHOOD NEWS ★ ★

Volume 2 . . . . A SPECIAL EDITION . . . . 50 cents

An Open-and-Shut Case

Sam Barr left his car in the Jiffy Burger lot while he ate lunch. When he returned to his car, he noticed that his suitcase was missing. People in the area reported seeing a tall red-headed man near Barr's car. Barr described the contents of his suitcase to the police. It contained his clothes, some newspapers, and a *large tarantula!*

Writing Fun: *Describe the possible reactions of the red-headed man when he later opened Barr's suitcase.*

★ ★ THE NEIGHBORHOOD NEWS ★ ★

Volume 1 .... A SPECIAL EDITION .... 50 cents

Monkey Puts People into Cage

A large monkey in the Knoxville Zoo escaped earlier today and chased several people into his cage. The monkey ripped the back metal wall from his cage and began running wildly through the crowds. Some of the frightened people stepped into the cage in order to get away from the crazed animal. The zoo owners quickly chased the animal and put it to sleep. No injuries were reported.

Writing Fun: *Write a story one of these people might have told to family members that night after returning home safely.*

★ ★ THE NEIGHBORHOOD NEWS ★ ★

Volume 2 .... A SPECIAL EDITION .... 50 cents

A Pair of Parakeets?

Betty Jones wanted to make sure that her pet parakeet, Pepperina, would be cared for after she died. She thought Pepperina might be happy with another parakeet as a friend. Yesterday Ms. Jones placed an ad in *The Neighborhood News* for a lifetime friend for Pepperina. She offered $10,000 to the owners of the selected bird.

Many area parakeet owners reported an interest in introducing their pets to Pepperina. Ms. Jones stated that Pepperina had been her only friend during the last few years of her life. She wanted to make sure Pepperina was provided for properly.

Writing Fun: *Pretend you are a parakeet owner. Tell how you might convince Ms. Jones that your parakeet should be the one selected as Pepperina's friend.*

★ ★ THE NEIGHBORHOOD NEWS ★ ★

Volume 1 . . . . A SPECIAL EDITION . . . . 50 cents

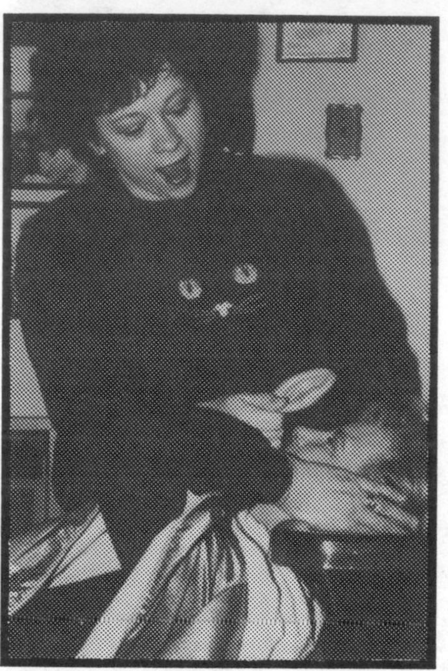

Woman Scrubs Lady's Ear Off

Sue Baldwin was having her hair washed at Joy's Beauty Shop yesterday. Suddenly her ear fell off into the hands of the shop's owner.

Owner Joy Ward was stunned. Ms. Baldwin, however, quickly informed her that it was an artificial one. She had earlier been in a car accident and afterwards had to have a special ear made for her which could be glued onto the side of her head.

"Some people have false teeth. I have a false ear," she joked. Ms. Ward, however, decided to scrub a little more carefully in the future.

Writing Fun: *Explain another funny scene which might occur with Ms. Baldwin because of her false ear.*

★ ★ THE NEIGHBORHOOD NEWS ★ ★

Volume 2 . . . . A SPECIAL EDITION . . . . 50 cents

Octogenarians Marry

Mabel Lee and Carey Rowe were "sweethearts" almost sixty-five years ago, but they each married someone else. Last May they met again at a home of a friend. Next week the couple, both now single and in their eighties, plan to wed.

Writing Fun: *An **octogenarian** is someone in his or her eighties. Pretend you are eighty, and single. You are planning to marry someone you **now** know. Give the details.*

★ ★ THE NEIGHBORHOOD NEWS ★ ★

Volume 1 . . . . A SPECIAL EDITION . . . . 50 cents

Elephant's Tooth Removed

Lillie, an old African elephant, had quit eating. The zoo owners thought that Lillie might not be able to chew or swallow her food because of a bad tooth.

An "elephant doctor" used a large hammer to remove the five-pound (2.25 kg) impacted tooth. Before he removed the tooth, however, the doctor made sure that Lillie was heavily sedated!

Writing Fun: *If Lillie could talk, how do you think she might describe her experience with her bad tooth?*

★ ★ THE NEIGHBORHOOD NEWS ★ ★

Volume 2 . . . . A SPECIAL EDITION . . . . 50 cents

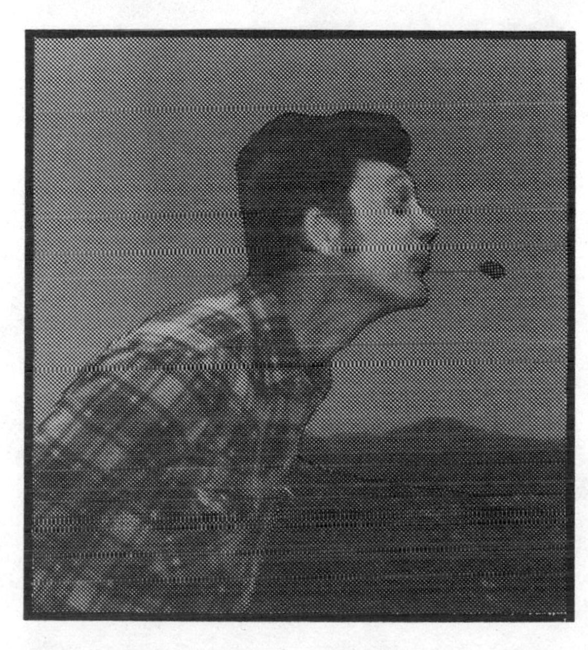

The Champion Cherry-Pit Spitter

A contest is held each year in Chicago to see who can spit cherry pits the greatest distance. Last week Jim Wills spit a cherry pit over sixty feet (18.24 m) away.

Several of his friends think they can beat his record before next year's event.

Writing Fun: *Write a tongue twister which could be used to describe this cherry-pit spitting contest.*

★ ★ THE NEIGHBORHOOD NEWS ★ ★

Volume 1 . . . . A SPECIAL EDITION . . . . 50 cents

Basketball Player Scores 156 Points

Marie Boyd Eichler scored 156 points in one basketball game between two Maryland high school rivals. That was almost sixty years ago, but the record has never been surpassed by either male or female. Marie successfully shot seventy-seven baskets and two free throws. The game score was 163-3.

Many of the rules of basketball have changed since that time. Marie did not pursue a career in basketball. Instead, she became a teacher.

Writing Fun: *Tell how you think the losing team felt when they only scored **three** points during the entire game as the winning team scored **163** points.*

★ ★ THE NEIGHBORHOOD NEWS ★ ★

Volume 2 . . . . A SPECIAL EDITION . . . . 50 cents

Monkey Stops Robbery

When Ann Rice was home alone last Thursday evening, she heard loud knocks at her door. Two men asked if they could use her telephone to report an automobile accident. After they entered the Rice home, they demanded her money and jewelry. As Ms. Rice started to hand them her purse, Cheeka, her pet monkey, jumped onto the shoulders of one robber, leaving a deep wound in his left jaw.When Cheeka headed for the other intruder, both uninvited guests made a quick escape.

Later Ms. Rice remarked that she had never known her monkey to bite anyone, although she now felt safer.

Writing Fun: *Tell how you think Ms. Rice will react he next time she hears someone knocking on her door.*

★ ★ THE NEIGHBORHOOD NEWS ★ ★

Volume 1 .... A SPECIAL EDITION .... 50 cents

The Tall Basketball Player

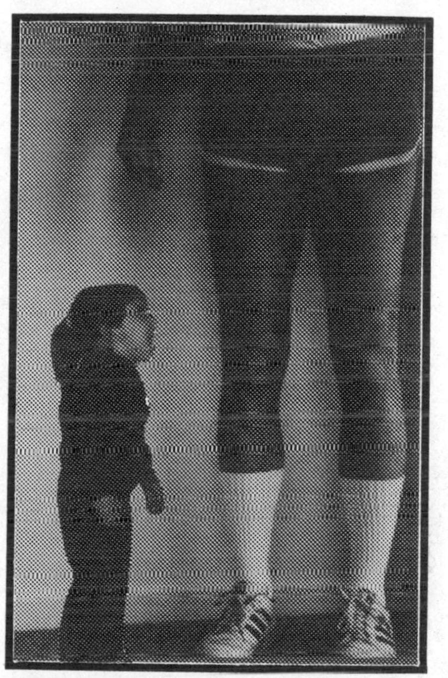

Chuck Nivett, a seven-foot-five (226 cm) basketball star, says that interesting things happen to him when he shops. Small children often walk up to him and stare. Some reach out to touch him to see if he is real. Many children find themselves staring at his knees. One child bit his leg and quickly ran behind a counter.

Nivett says that being tall, however, does have some good points. He has had a very successful basketball career.

Writing Fun: *This tall man suggested that being tall has some good points. Describe one case where being very, very tall could be quite helpful to someone.*

★ ★ THE NEIGHBORHOOD NEWS ★ ★

Volume 2 .... A SPECIAL EDITION .... 50 cents

Man Sits in Tub of Wet Spaghetti

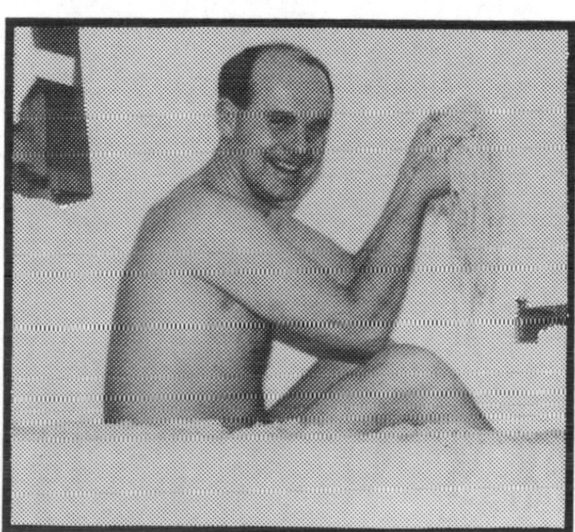

C. R. Stewart claims the world's record for sitting the longest time in a tub of wet spaghetti. Friends reported that he stayed there for over fifty-three hours. Each hour he took a ten-minute break. Then he returned to the tub of cold, wet spaghetti.

After he claimed the record, he took a very long shower. He wondered if he would ever be able to eat spaghetti again.

Writing Fun: *Pretend you are Mr. Stewart. The contest is over. You have arrived at a friend's house for dinner. Spaghetti will be the main course. Describe how you might react.*

★ ★ THE NEIGHBORHOOD NEWS ★ ★

Volume 1 .... A SPECIAL EDITION .... 50 cents

Pie Attempt Flops

A cherry pie, baked in honor of George Washington's birthday, *almost* made it. The pie measured ten feet across the top and twelve inches deep. As the bakers tried to load the baked pie onto a truck, the pie fell into the parking lot.

Rather than winning the record for the world's largest pie, they laughed about having the world's stickiest parking lot. Smaller pies were quickly baked to replace the large one.

***Writing Fun:** You have been told to clean up this parking lot after this "accident." Tell how you might get this job done.*

★ ★ THE NEIGHBORHOOD NEWS ★ ★

Volume 2 .... A SPECIAL EDITION .... 50 cents

The Panda Wedding

The zookeeper at the Bamboo Zoo wanted to have some fun. He decided that "Paul," a male panda in his zoo, and "Paula," a female panda, should get married.

As a joke he sent wedding announcements to many people in the town. On the wedding day over thirty people watched the panda wedding. One person even brought them a gift.

***Writing Fun:** Prepare a printed wedding invitation which this zookeeper could have used for this occasion.*

★ ★ THE NEIGHBORHOOD NEWS ★ ★

Volume 1 .... A SPECIAL EDITION .... 50 cents

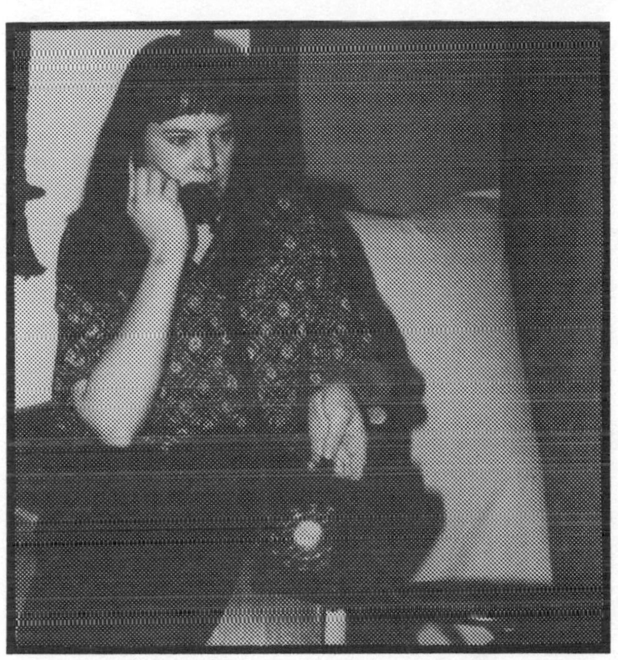

Water Bed Fills Room

Yesterday Mary Clay turned on the water to fill her water bed. Then her best friend phoned to chat. Mary forgot about the water. When she returned to her bedroom, the water bed had expanded to fill the entire room.

The firemen came to rescue Ms. Clay from her near disaster. They told her she was lucky it had not burst.

Writing Fun: *Ms. Clay's best friend is now calling her again. Write a conversation they might have.*

★ ★ THE NEIGHBORHOOD NEWS ★ ★

Volume 2 .... A SPECIAL EDITION .... 50 cents

Dog Drives Police Car

Roger Cox, a city policeman, rushed to find out who had driven his car into a parked truck. Cox found the "driver" sitting behind the wheel, panting. The "driver" was his dog, Copper.

Cox and Copper were riding down Main Street when Cox saw a truck go through a red light. He chased the truck. When it stopped, Cox got out of his car. He left it running. A few minutes later he heard a loud noise. The truck was shaking. He decided that Copper must have hit the gear shift and moved it from park into drive.

There was no damage.

Writing Fun: *Since Copper caused a traffic accident, perhaps he should be given a ticket. Design and fill out a "ticket" which you think should be given to this dog.*

★ ★ THE NEIGHBORHOOD NEWS ★ ★
Volume 1 .... A SPECIAL EDITION .... 50 cents

★ ★ THE NEIGHBORHOOD NEWS ★ ★
Volume 2 .... A SPECIAL EDITION .... 50 cents

CLASSROOM BOOKLETS

The process of teaching writing has many styles. One suggested style for the following provided patterns is to display a selected design which will be used as an outside cover of a classroom booklet. Read aloud to the class one of the provided activities in **Step 5** for this design. Have each student write a response for this activity. Place these responses together to make a classroom booklet. The design itself may be used as the cover sheet for the complete packet of writing responses.

Note that any form of individual or small group writing activity may also occur with these designs and activities.

These provided designs are grouped as follows for use with various occasions:

HALLOWEEN:

OH, NO! (Ghost)
My Nine Lives (Cat)
The Spell (Witch)
The Brew (Kettle)
The Happy Jack-O'-Lantern
The Angry Jack-O'-Lantern

THANKSGIVING:

HELP! (Turkey)
The Youngest Pilgrim

CHRISTMAS:

The Smallest Reindeer
Santa's Substitute
The Barest Christmas Tree Ever
The Stocking Surprise
The Lazy Elf

WINTER:

Cool It! (Snowman)

VALENTINE'S DAY:

Cupid's Goof!
The Broken Heart

EASTER:

The Rabbit Habit

OTHER OCCASIONS:

The Unusual Leprechaun
What YOU Can Do for America

GENERAL:

The Joyrider
The Castle Adventure
The Drink
A Good Sport
The Broken Window
The Strange Computer

DESIGNS FOR LITERATURE:

Wilbur's Woes
Charlotte's Challenges

Numerous writing activities may occur with these designs. The following provides writing suggestions for various stages in the Five-Step Writing Plan described on page 6. Step 5 may result in the classroom booklets. Any of the suggestions for Steps 1-4 may **precede** this in order to help improve the quality of the final writing product.

OH, NO! (Ghost)

STEP 1—THE WORD: What are some words which might describe how this ghost feels?

STEP 2—THE PHRASE: Select two of these words and place in front of the word *ghost*. An example is *the terrified, nervous ghost.*

STEP 3—THE SENTENCE: Write one sentence which tells how this ghost might feel.

STEP 4—THE PARAGRAPH: Write one paragraph explaining what might scare a ghost.

STEP 5—THE STORY: Finish the following story:

Ghasty Ghost had lived in the old abandoned Frankenhyde mansion for over a hundred years. Each year a few of the neighborhood children trudged up the long hill to the mansion to try to spend Halloween night there. Almost always they had been dared to do so by older children. Sometimes Ghasty overheard an amount of money they had been offered if they could actually stay there the entire night.

Each year around midnight, Ghasty made his usual appearance. He never said "Boo!" In fact, he never said anything. He just clumsily came down the attic stairs and opened the creaky door. Then he heard the terrifying screams of the visitors, followed by the scurrying sounds of their departure.

"It's so easy," thought Ghasty. "All I ever do is walk down the stairs."

Generally no one ever came back until the next Halloween. Therefore, Ghasty took some long naps, sometimes for a year at a time. This caused him to miss most of the neighborhood news.

Ghasty's Halloween this year might have been different had he **not** slept through the entire previous year. He had not heard that the Nerdmans had moved close by. There were thirteen Nerdman children, and **all thirteen** had been dared to spend the night in the old mansion. . . .

My Nine Lives (Cat)

STEP 1—THE WORD: What are some words which might describe cats that are household pets? What are some words which might describe cats in general? What words might describe the cat in this picture?

STEP 2—THE PHRASE: Select any two of these words and place in front of the word *cat*.

STEP 3—THE SENTENCE: Look into the eyes of this cat. Write a thought it could be having. Be sure to enclose these words in quotation marks.

STEP 4—THE PARAGRAPH: The saying "a cat has nine lives" has been in existence for many decades. Write one paragraph explaining how you think this saying might have started.

STEP 5—THE STORY: Finish one of the following stories:

Choice A: Katherine Kat had used up eight of her lives! She knew she must proceed cautiously for a long time. She began to tiptoe everywhere instead of going full speed ahead. She started examining her food before she ate it. She peered suspiciously ahead every few feet. Before long, her day was filled with lurking, suspecting, and avoiding. Then one day. . . .

Choice B: Write a biography of a famous cat. Divide this biography into nine sections—one for each of its lives.

The Spell (Witch)

STEP 1—THE WORD: What are some words which might describe witches in general? What are some words which might describe this witch?

STEP 2—THE PHRASE: Give this witch a name. Select two words and place in front of this witch's name.

STEP 3—THE SENTENCE: Write one sentence which describes what this witch looks like.

STEP 4—THE PARAGRAPH: Write one paragraph which explains how a make-believe witch might be able to cast a spell on someone.

STEP 5—THE STORY: Finish this story: The witch at Cobbler's Creek had decided to cast a spell on little Joey. She had never liked him since his family moved to the edge of the creek. The time was now. First she. . . .

The Brew (Kettle)

STEP 1—THE WORD: Have you ever tasted a beverage which someone called *witches' brew?* If so, what words would you use to describe how it tasted? If not, how do you think it might taste?

STEP 2—THE PHRASE: What phrases would you use to describe a brew which you think should be served in your school's cafeteria at Halloween?

STEP 3—THE SENTENCE: Write one sentence which describes **who** should make such brew.

STEP 4—THE PARAGRAPH: Write one paragraph telling **how** you think such brew should be made.

STEP 5—THE STORY: Finish one of the following stories:

Choice A: Witch Howeena began making a batch of Halloween brew. She had all the usual ingredients that witches generally put in their brew. Then she had an idea. **Her** brew for this Halloween was going to be ***different!*** First she decided to. . . .

Choice B: Jerry was now next in line. He was already having second thoughts. He wanted to join the ***Wrathscare*** club, but to become a member he would have to drink one **full** cup of their special Halloween brew. The club leader handed Jerry his cup.

Suddenly Jerry. . . .

The Happy Jack-O'-Lantern
The Angry Jack-O'-Lantern

STEP 1—THE WORD: Write some words which are synonyms for *happy*. Write some words which are synonyms for *angry*.

STEP 2—THE PHRASE: Write one phrase which describes one part of the Jack-O'-Lantern's face.

STEP 3—THE SENTENCE: Write one sentence telling whether you would rather meet a happy Jack-O'-Lantern or an angry Jack-O'-Lantern.

STEP 4—THE PARAGRAPH: Have you ever wondered why the name *Jack* is used in the name of this character? Write a paragraph explaining why *Jack* should be changed to another name for this Halloween character.

STEP 5—THE STORY: Select one of the following choices for a story:

Choice A: Look in an encyclopedia or other book to find how this Halloween character began. Write a story about this character.

Choice B: A smile is usually carved onto the face of most Jack-O'-Lanterns. Write a story about why you think someone might have carved a sad face instead of a smile.

HELP! (Turkey)

STEP 1—THE WORD: If a turkey knew it was going to be eaten on Thanksgiving Day, what are some words which could describe how it might feel?

STEP 2—THE PHRASE: The word *turkey* is used at times to describe a person. Write a phrase which could describe this same type of person.

STEP 3—THE SENTENCE: Write a sentence which could describe another problem a turkey might face other than being eaten on Thanksgiving Day.

STEP 4—THE PARAGRAPH: Write a rhythmical paragraph which could be a plea expressed by a turkey at Thanksgiving time. One sample is "All us turkeys would like to say, 'Please have ham on Thanksgiving Day!'"

STEP 5—THE STORY: Finish one of the following stories:

Choice A: Timmy Turkey had just heard the bad news. The family was planning to have either ham or turkey this year for Thanksgiving dinner. He was now the ***only*** turkey left on the farm. Phillip, the only pig on the farm, was a family favorite. Timmy felt that Phillip would certainly not be eaten for Thanksgiving dinner. Timmy began to sweat! He knew he must devise a plan. First, he. . . .

Choice B: An evil witch had cast a spell on Jason. She had turned him into a turkey. For one year he would continue to look and act just like a turkey. It was miserable eating food with a beak and scratching around the barnyard all day. Jason had counted the days. Only one month was left. Just then he heard Farmer Cox open the gate. He noticed that he was carrying an ax. Jason suddenly remembered that Thanksgiving was approaching. . . .

The Youngest Pilgrim

STEP 1—THE WORD: Make a list of words which could be used to describe the early pilgrims in our country.

STEP 2—THE PHRASE: Select two of these words and place in front of the word *pilgrim.*

STEP 3—THE SENTENCE: Write a one-sentence description of one problem which the early pilgrims might have faced.

STEP 4—THE PARAGRAPH: Write a paragraph explaining a solution to this problem.

STEP 5—THE STORY: Finish one of the following stories:

Choice A: All of us Pilgrims and Indians are planning a big feast today. You should see the food! Some of it really looks terrific. Some of it, however, doesn't look quite so scrumptious. Let me describe it for you. . . .

Choice B: I wonder why I have to wear such a crazy looking hat like this. What if the Indians had to wear such a ridiculous garment? Just look at the bright and colorful ones they get to wear! Maybe I could just swap with them for a while. . . .

Choice C: Mom and Dad told me that my life would be so much better here in America than it would have been where I was born. So they sent me on a ship called the *Mayflower* with a bunch of other people. Here I am now in America. I wonder. . . .

The Smallest Reindeer

STEP 1—THE WORD: What are some words which could be used to describe reindeer?

STEP 2—THE PHRASE: Place two of these words in front of the word *reindeer.*

STEP 3—THE SENTENCE: Write one sentence which describes the reindeer in this picture.

STEP 4—THE PARAGRAPH: Write a paragraph telling whether or not you think reindeer are real creatures. Why or why not?

STEP 5—THE STORY: Finish one of the following stories:

Choice A: It was the young reindeer's first Christmas.

"How exciting!" he exclaimed. "I will get to help deliver all of the presents this year."

"Just a minute," protested Rudolph. . . .

Choice B: "Hey, Dad, may I borrow the sleigh tonight?" young Rudolph asked as his dad was finishing some of the chores. "It is still a few days before you need it for the Christmas haul, and I would like to go over and see Darla Deer."

The elder Rudolph stopped his chores. He gazed at the ground for a few moments.

"Son," he began. . . .

Santa's Substitute

STEP 1—THE WORD: What are some words which could be used as synonyms for the word *substitute*?

STEP 5—THE STORY: Finish this story: "Santa is very sick!" announced Mrs. Claus with tears in her eyes. "He won't be able to make the rounds tonight to take toys and presents to all the boys and girls in the land!"

All in Santa Land began to cry. They couldn't bear the thoughts of all the broken hearts this would cause.

"Wait a minute!" said a small voice coming from the back of the room. "I can substitute for Santa this year. Here is my plan. . . .

The Barest Christmas Tree Ever

STEP 1—THE WORD: Make a list of words which could be used to describe a *bare* tree.

STEP 2—THE PHRASE: Use some of these words in a phrase to describe a Christmas tree.

STEP 4—THE PARAGRAPH: Write a paragraph to explain why someone might have a bare Christmas tree.

STEP 5—THE STORY: Finish one of the following stories:

Choice A: The Birdmans had no money for Christmas this year. Mr. Birdman had lost his job and Mrs. Birdman was very ill.

"There will be no presents under our tree this year," little Jamie said softly.

"I don't even call this a tree," replied Jerry, Jamie's older brother. They both looked at the drab tree sparsely covered with the remains of last year's decorations.

Just then the doorbell rang at the Birdman residence. What happened next changed the lives of each member of the family. . . .

Choice B: Each of the animals in Wandering Forest decided to celebrate Christmas this year in the same manner as they had observed "people" celebrate it in the past.

"First, we must get a tree," exclaimed Mrs. Beaver.

"Let us help," chimed in all the little beavers.

So the beaver family began. . . .

The Stocking Surprise

STEP 1—THE WORD: Make a list of items which you would like to have placed in a stocking for you.

STEP 2—THE PHRASE: Select one of these items and add two words to describe it.

STEP 3—THE SENTENCE: Write one sentence describing an item you would place in the stocking for one of your parents.

STEP 4—THE PARAGRAPH: The custom of having Christmas stockings has existed in America for many decades. Write a paragraph explaining how this custom began. Use an encyclopedia for this information if you wish.

STEP 5—THE STORY: Finish one of these stories:

Choice A: It **looked** just like all the other stockings hanging by the fireplace. No one would ever guess what might actually be inside. . . .

Choice B: The stocking was actually **crying!** The toy soldier stuffed inside heard the sobs and asked, "Why are you crying, Stocking? I didn't even know stockings *could* cry."

"After Christmas I will be stored back in the box with all the other decorations," said the stocking. "You will get to stay out and play with all the children. It will be one year before I will get to see anyone again."

"I had never thought about that," answered the toy soldier. "But I have an idea. After you have been emptied on Christmas day, why don't you sneak away and crawl into the family sock drawer? No one will miss you since there are so many stockings this year. Then maybe someone in the family will start **wearing** you."

"What a good idea!" exclaimed the stocking. And on Christmas day he did just that! But what a surprise awaited him. . . .

The Lazy Elf

STEP 1—THE WORD: Make a list of words which are synonyms for the word *lazy*.

STEP 3—THE SENTENCE: Write a sentence describing someone you know who is lazy.

STEP 4—THE PARAGRAPH: Write one paragraph which describes the laziest **you** have ever been.

STEP 5—THE STORY: Finish one of the following stories:

Choice A: "I **refuse** to help make that toy for children this year," protested one of Santa's elves.

"Why?" asked the other elves.

"It is too much work!" the lazy elf explained.

"Oh, no!" explained another elf. "Without **that** toy. . . .

Choice B: "Why aren't you working?" Santa asked the elf whom he had found sitting in the corner of the room.

"I'll tell you why," began the elf. "Some of us have harder jobs than others and it is just not fair. Besides that, we are all paid the same even though some of us are much better than others! It's just not fair!"

"In that case, I have a plan," answered Santa.

Santa's plan changed everything that Christmas. . . .

Cool It! (Snowman)

STEP 1—THE WORD: Make a list of words which could describe a snowman.

STEP 2—THE PHRASE: Place two of these words in front of the word *snowman*.

STEP 3—THE SENTENCE: Write a sentence telling what you would put on the head of a snowman as decoration.

STEP 4—THE PARAGRAPH: Write a paragraph telling how you would decorate the face of a snowman using only items in your room at home.

STEP 5—THE STORY: Finish one of the following stories:

Choice A: As a snowman, my life can be very exciting! I have many friends and I have great adventures. But I have several problems, too. **Heat** is my worst enemy. Each day the sun shines I become weaker and weaker. The sun completely destroyed my older brother last month. I don't want it to destroy me, so I must think of a solution. . . .

Choice B: Some folks think that I am not real and that I cannot talk. However, I **am** real and I can and do talk to all creatures except humans. Sometimes, however, these conversations frighten me! Just last week I talked with. . . .

Cupid's Goof!

STEP 1—THE WORD: What are some other words which could be used instead of the word *goof?*

STEP 2—THE PHRASE: Write a title of a book which might contain the word *goof.*

STEP 3—THE SENTENCE: Write a sentence describing Cupid.

STEP 4—THE PARAGRAPH: Write a paragraph explaining the biggest goof you have ever made.

STEP 5—THE STORY: Finish one of the following stories:

Choice A: Cupid was at work again! He had such a splendid idea to match up a certain boy and girl. It all seemed right. There was one important thing, however, that Cupid didn't know about **this** boy and girl. . . .

Choice B: A friend of the opposite sex has been calling you at your home quite often. You are not at all interested in developing a friendship with this person. Tell what you plan to do.

The Broken Heart

STEP 1—THE WORD: Those who experience a "broken heart" have different kinds of feelings. Make a list of words which help explain such feelings.

STEP 2—THE PHRASE: Name three things which might have caused heartbreak for others which will ***never*** break ***your*** heart.

STEP 3—THE SENTENCE: Hearts can "break" for reasons other than love. Explain one possible example of this type of heartbreak.

STEP 4—THE PARAGRAPH: Write a paragraph telling about one of your own greatest heartbreaks.

STEP 5—THE STORY: Finish one of the following stories:

Choice A: Barbara looked at her older brother. He had arrived home early and was sitting on the sofa gazing solemnly at the ceiling. A single tear forced its way down his cheek—then another, and another. She wished she could ease his pain. Then she recalled a multitude of naughty pranks he had played on her. She slowly stepped into the room. . . .

Choice B: Sarah watched as Jim lifted his tray in the cafeteria line. She gazed at his slow steady stride toward his table. He had never expressed an interest in her. So she decided that it was not up to **her.** She would tell **him** how much she really cared about him. She walked slowly toward his table. . . .

The Rabbit Habit

STEP 1—THE WORD: What are some words which are synonyms for *habit?*

STEP 2—THE PHRASE: Make a list of habits that are annoying to you.

STEP 3—THE SENTENCE: Write a sentence which explains a **good** habit to have.

STEP 4—THE PARAGRAPH: Write a paragraph about how you would plan to **change** your worst habit.

STEP 5—THE STORY: Finish one of the following stories:

Choice A: Robbie Rabbit had a habit of coloring Easter eggs for all the boys and girls in his village. However, this year something changed. . . .

Choice B: Write a story about an unusual "Easter Bunny."

The Unusual Leprechaun

STEP 1—THE WORD: A Leprechaun is a mythical being which is used as a character in many folklore stories, particularly those from Ireland. Make a list of other mythical beings.

STEP 5—THE STORY: Finish one of the following stories:

Choice A: Michael McReady, a 300-year-old leprechaun, has decided to retire. Since Michael always wanted an education, he has enrolled at **your** school! As he walks into your classroom, he takes the only empty seat which is the one immediately behind you. Tell about some things which might happen while Michael is sitting behind you in school.

Choice B: George's luck had suddenly run out. He didn't know where to turn. Everything bad and rotten had happened to him just within the last few days. He decided to run away from home. He packed a few clothes and a small amount of food, then tiptoed out his back door. Just as he walked down the last step, a leprechaun appeared. . . .

Choice C: You have just arrived at school and heard that your class will have a substitute for that day. As everyone settles down, the substitute walks into your room. It is a leprechaun. Tell what you think will happen in today's class.

Choice D: Patrick O'Teary is moving away from Ireland. Patrick is tired of being a leprechaun and has decided to become a "person" in America. He is not sure, however, if he will be able to disguise himself well enough. Tell about his possible experiences in America.

Choice E: Are leprechauns real? If you caught one, would he reveal to you the hiding place of a great treasure? Pretend you have caught one and you intend to coax him into telling you where a treasure is hidden. Relate the conversation you plan to have with him **and** tell of your adventure in attempting to locate the treasure.

What YOU Can Do for America

STEP 1—THE WORD: List some words which are synonyms for *freedom.*

STEP 2—THE PHRASE: If you were writing a new national anthem for our country, what are some phrases you would want to include?

STEP 3—THE SENTENCE: Write one sentence which might be in this new anthem.

STEP 4—THE PARAGRAPH: Write a paragraph telling why you would (or would not) want to move away from America permanently.

STEP 5—THE STORY: Finish the following story:

The United States President has called on **you** for advice. The advice you give him can change the lives of many Americans.

Tell what his question is for you and give your answer. Explain the reasons for your answer.

The Joyrider

STEP 1—THE WORD: A vehicle is sometimes referred to as a joyrider. What are some other words a vehicle could be called?

STEP 2—THE PHRASE: If **your** car is called a joyrider, write a phrase which would describe this vehicle.

STEP 3—THE SENTENCE: Write a sentence stating a problem we might have if there were no cars.

STEP 4—THE PARAGRAPH: Write an ad for the local newspaper which might be used to sell the car a member of your family currently owns.

STEP 5—THE STORY: Finish one of the following stories:

Choice A: You are a car which has been personally owned by a famous movie star. You have accompanied this star on many long and interesting trips. Choose **one** of these trips and tell the details.

Choice B: Three cars were waiting beneath the red light at the six-lane intersection. All engines roared with a force that vibrated the pavement for several blocks. Each driver glanced at the others while waiting for the precise moment the green light would flicker, signaling their chance for a departure which would decide once and for all. . . .

Choice C: The sixteenth birthday of your close friend has finally arrived. He has looked forward to this day for years, primarily because he will be able to **drive!** He has invited you to go for a "cruise" with him. He is now at your house, ready to pick you up. . . .

Choice D: Step right up, folks! See this beautiful, almost-new, jazzy sports model. The single owner of today's special buy was Miss Simpleton, one of the town's lovely teachers, who walked everywhere rather than risk getting her car muddy and dirty. Let me tell you about this marvelous bargain. . . .

The Castle Adventure

STEP 1—THE WORD: What are some words which would describe a castle?

STEP 2—THE PHRASE: Write a phrase which would describe a castle.

STEP 3—THE SENTENCE: Write a sentence telling how many rooms a castle might have.

STEP 5—THE STORY: Finish one of the following stories:

Choice A: All of the animals of Mimwood Forest were tired of living without a roof over their heads. They decided to have the smartest of the forest creatures design and build a castle in which they all could live.

Decide which animals you think should design the castle and which ones should actually build it. Draw a floor plan for each level in the castle. Give each room a name and tell which animal(s) should live in each room.

Tell about one problem which might arise after all of the animals moved into the castle.

Choice B: Clyde and Carla were playing in their favorite spot in Central Park. Since Clyde was becoming a little bored with playing ball, he threw a high, wild toss to Carla. She ran to the park's edge to make the catch, but the ball landed beyond a tall tree. Both raced to recover the ball, but when they reached the other side of the tree, no ball was in sight. Slowly they searched deeper into the wooded area. As they passed through another small grove of trees, there ahead of them was a beautiful castle!

"I wonder who lives there," Carla exclaimed.

"Why don't we find out?" Clyde replied.

Both walked in the direction of the enormous castle. . . .

Choice C: No one had lived in the old abandoned castle for over thirty years. No one had even been seen on the grounds during that time. One night, however, things changed. Just a few minutes after midnight, a loud scream was heard. Raymond jumped out of bed and looked from his window in the direction of the old castle. A bright purple glow shone from one of the castle's upper windows. Raymond decided to sneak out of his house to investigate. . . .

Choice D: Edward and Paul were invited to spend the summer with Aunt Narnella. She lived all alone in a large castle deep in Elmwood Forest. The boys had never visited their aunt before, and they couldn't wait to explore the many rooms in her castle. Tell about one adventure you think they might have in this castle.

The Drink

STEP 1—THE WORD: If you could fill this glass with any beverage in the world, with the agreement that it would be the **only** liquid you could drink for one year, what choice would it be? What are some adjectives that would describe this choice?

STEP 2—THE PHRASE: Combine two of your selected adjectives with your choice of beverage and write a descriptive phrase for this drink.

STEP 5—THE STORY: Finish one of the following stories:

Choice A: You are baby-sitting for the neighborhood "punk." He has been playing with his chemistry set and is now holding a glass filled with a strange-looking liquid. You are watching him lift the glass to his lips. What will you do?

Choice B: The man tried to focus his eyes. The ceiling, the hospital walls, and a woman who appeared to be dressed as a nurse were blurry and swaying.

"What happened?" he mumbled. The words seemed to crack in his dry throat.

"Don't worry about it," the woman answered. "Just drink this."

She held the glass to his lips. . . .

Choice C: Karen was attending her first party for "couples." David, one of Central's most popular athletes, had invited her to the party. David generally took Angela, but Angela's parents had refused to let her attend this type of party. Karen felt fortunate that Angela's parents were so old-fashioned, although she had not been completely honest with her own parents regarding what type of party was planned. But when David phoned, she knew she **had** to go!

At the party Karen was surprised to discover that the others were much older than she had expected. She soon felt uneasy.

Her thoughts were interrupted when David handed her a glass.

"What is this?" Karen asked.

"Just drink it, and don't ask any questions," David snapped. . . .

Choice D: Fred had been captured by the Kryptanes. He was accused of attempting to steal their secret plans for the world's destruction. Fred knew of their method of determining guilt and its subsequent punishment. A strange glass was placed in front of the suspect. Only one swallow was necessary. After this swallow, the suspect, if guilty, would die a very slow and painful death. The Kryptanes believed that the liquid in the glass contained a substance which produced a poisonous reaction in the stomach of an individual who was **guilty** of an accusation. The innocent would experience no pain or discomfort. They had used this method for centuries and felt it had never failed them.

Fred was strapped to the chair. Only his right arm was free. The glass was placed before him.

"Drink," ordered their leader.

Fred slowly picked up the glass. . . .

A Good Sport

STEP 1—THE WORD: You are going to design a sport which will be played in the future. The first thing you must do is to **name** this sport. What are some names you could use?

STEP 2—THE PHRASE: Look at the guy in this picture. Write two adjectives and one noun which will fit this situation.

STEP 3—THE SENTENCE: The guy in this picture will be playing the new sport you have designed. Write a sentence which an announcer might use to introduce him.

STEP 4—THE PARAGRAPH: Write an ad for your local newspaper which could be used to advertise for a coach for this new sport.

STEP 5—THE STORY: Finish one of the following stories:

Choice A: Yesterday was Field Day at Tyson School. All students had been asked to come prepared to participate in a fun game of their favorite sport. The coach was going from room to room to see if anyone had forgotten to bring the needed equipment. As he arrived in Mr. Montgomery's room, he noticed. . . .

Choice B: George was already late for practice. His mother had insisted that he help his sister with the dishes, and now he was not going to be able to get to practice on time. He quickly opened his closet door to grab his gear. In his haste he grabbed some of the wrong pieces of equipment.

George had just arrived at practice when he noticed. . . .

Choice C: The phrase "a good sport" has more than one meaning. It can refer to having a good attitude about what you do, whether or not athletics are involved. It can also refer to athletics. Write a story which includes both of these meanings.

The Broken Window

STEP 5—THE STORY: Finish one of the following stories:

Choice A: Traci sat quietly in her room. Her door was closed in order to deafen the sounds of her parents' arguments. She had refused to eat her evening meal because of a quarrel with one of her friends. She felt all alone.

Suddenly she heard a loud crash. A small brick soared through her window. It tumbled to the edge of her bed. She examined it from a distance. A string joined both the brick and a small piece of heavy paper.

Shakily, she walked over and picked up the paper. . . .

Choice B: It was just too tempting for Sam. After all, the building had been abandoned for almost six months. He just had to see how high he could throw a rock. All those panes of glass were just waiting for action! No one would ever know. . . .

Choice C: Charles and Sean wanted to practice for the baseball tryouts. All the practice fields were taken, so they decided to practice in the Bakers' backyard. No one in the Baker family would be home early, so no one would be disturbed.

They didn't **intend** to bat, just catch. Catching, however, soon became boring, so they thought they would practice bunting. Bunting soon became boring also, and before long. . . .

Choice D: You have been placed on a committee to help decide upon punishments for misbehaviors of the students at your school. Your closest friend has broken a window in the school cafeteria. He described the situation as accidental. Miss Tallyhoe, the cafeteria supervisor, however, described the event as "a deliberate attempt to deface school property." The hearing is about to begin. Write an account of what you think will happen.

Choice E: Your little brother has broken a window in your home. Your parents will be so angry that they will ground him for a month. He is **begging** you to help him "cover up" until he can get someone to fix the window. Explain what you will do.

The Strange Computer

STEP 1—THE WORD: The computer in this picture was described as *strange*. What words would you use to describe computers you have seen?

STEP 2—THE PHRASE: Select some of these words to write one phrase to describe a computer.

STEP 3—THE SENTENCE: In one sentence describe a computer you would like to own.

STEP 4—THE PARAGRAPH: Write a paragraph describing what you think computers will be like ten years from now.

STEP 5—THE STORY: Finish one of the following stories:

Choice A: As Jim sat at his desk, he heard a strange noise. It was a voice coming from inside his computer. . . .

Choice B: It was huge! It had flashing lights! It was green! It was a strange computer. . . .

Note: The following two designs and examples are to be used after the learners have read the book ***Charlotte's Web.*** Other books and stories may be used in the same manner for similar writing experiences.

Wilbur's Woes

STEP 1—THE WORD: What words could be used to describe Wilbur *before* Charlotte was able to help him? What words could be used to describe him *after* she helped solve his problem?

STEP 2—THE PHRASE: Write a phrase which describes Wilbur at any point in the book.

STEP 3—THE SENTENCE: Compare Wilbur to a person you know.

STEP 4—THE PARAGRAPH: If Charlotte had not been able to help Wilbur, what solution would **you** have offered him?

STEP 5—THE STORY: Finish one of the following stories:

Choice A: Wilbur faced many "woes" in the book ***Charlotte's Web.*** His life, however, was not over when the book ended. He still may face several additional adventures. Write about one adventure which you think he may face which might be *woeful* to him.

Choice B: During Wilbur's lifetime he became quite experienced with expressing emotions we typically attribute to **people.** *Sorrow* was one example. Make a list of other emotions you think Wilbur learned how to express. Write a brief story about why Wilbur **did** or **would** express one of these emotions.

Charlotte's Challenges

STEP 1—THE WORD: What words could be used to describe Charlotte?

STEP 2—THE PHRASE: Write a phrase which describes Charlotte near the end of this story.

STEP 3—THE SENTENCE: Write a sentence about Charlotte in which several of the words begin with **ch.**

STEP 4—THE PARAGRAPH: Much could be learned about spiders from this book. Write a paragraph containing only factual information you learned about spiders.

STEP 5—THE STORY: Finish one of the following stories:

Choice A: In the book ***Charlotte's Web,*** Charlotte had many challenges. Which one of her challenges do you feel was the most difficult? Tell why you feel as you do.

Choice B: Prior to meeting Wilbur, Charlotte had faced many other challenges. Pretend **you** are Charlotte and you are planning to appear on a television talk show. You will be discussing your greatest challenge **prior** to meeting Willbur. What will you say?

Note: The above examples provide specific instances of how the Five-Step Writing Plan can be implemented. A multitude of different designs may be used in the same manner. Pictures from magazines and newspapers may further provide materials for this use. Two additional sources of such designs are ***Creative Writing Booklets*** and ***#2 Creative Writing Booklets*** also published by Good Apple. Both of these books contain full and half-page designs with accompanying activities for these levels of writing.

OH,
NO!

My Nine
Lives

The Spell

THE
BREW

The Happy Jack-O'-Lantern

The Angry Jack-O'-Lantern

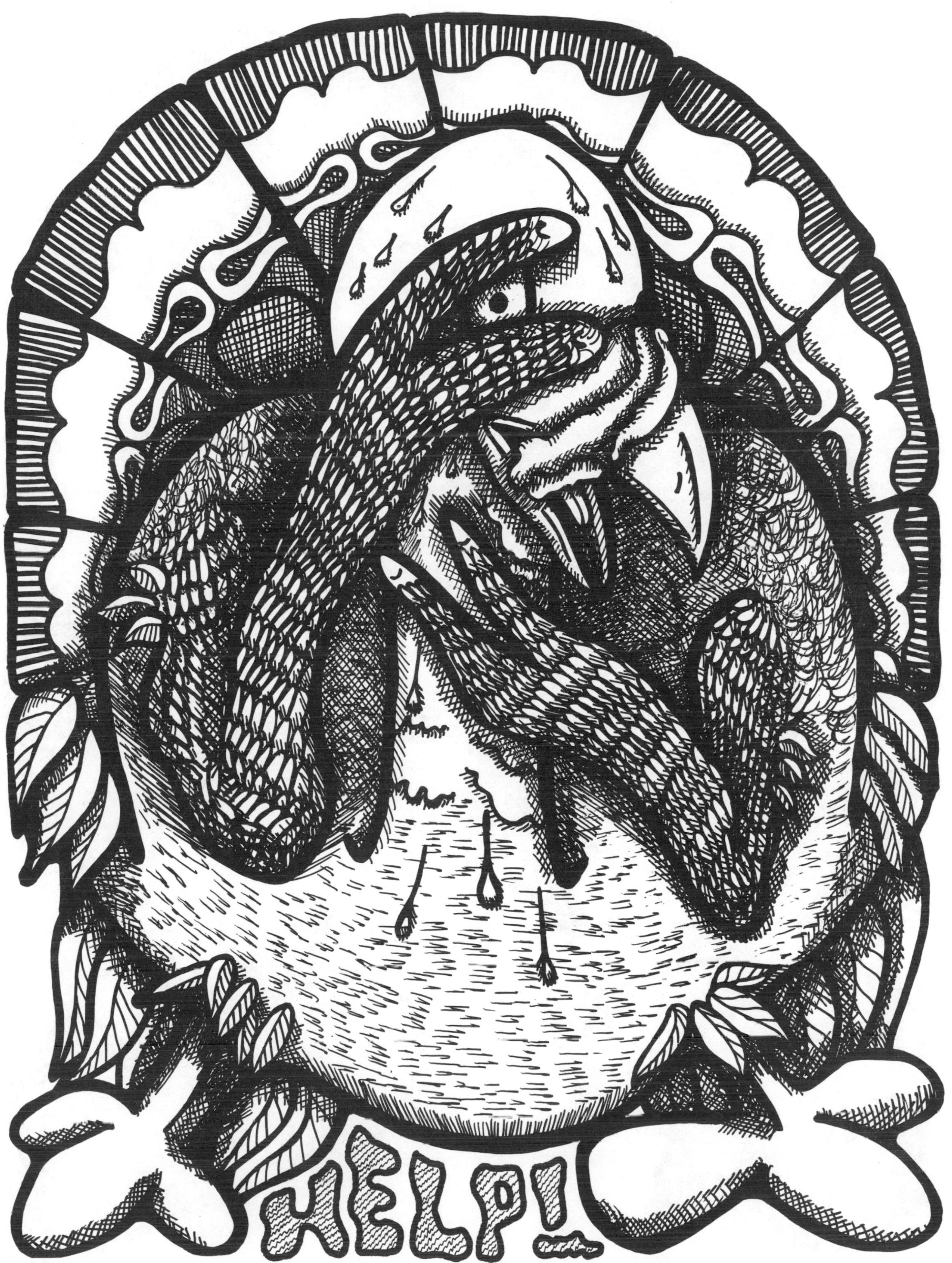
HELP!

THE
YOUNGEST
PILGRIM

The
Smallest
Reindeer

Santa's Substitute

The Barest
Christmas Tree Ever
Pat Harroll

The
Stocking
Surprise

The
Lazy
Elf

Cool
It!

Cupid's
Goof!

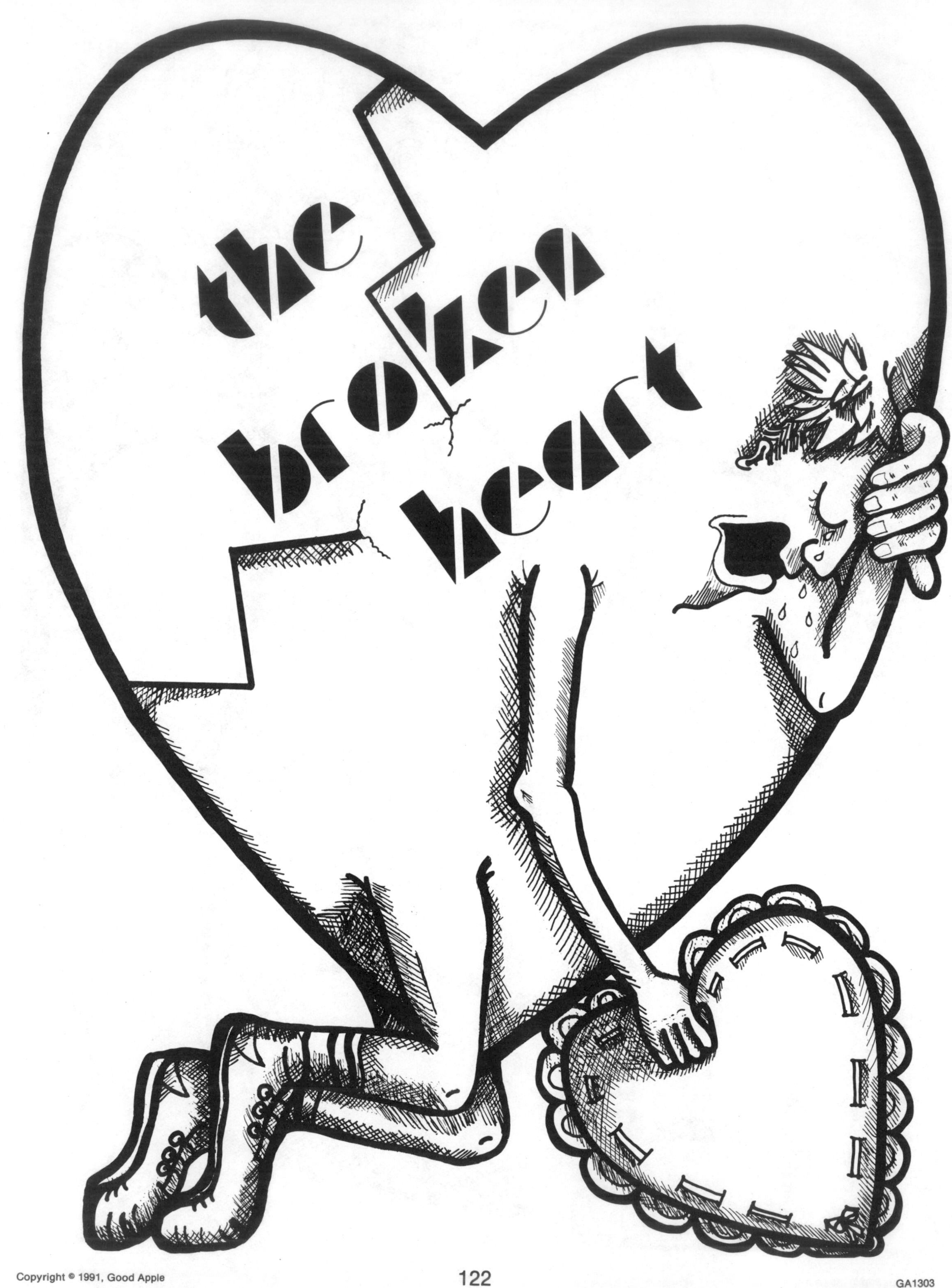
the
broken
heart

The Rabbit Habit

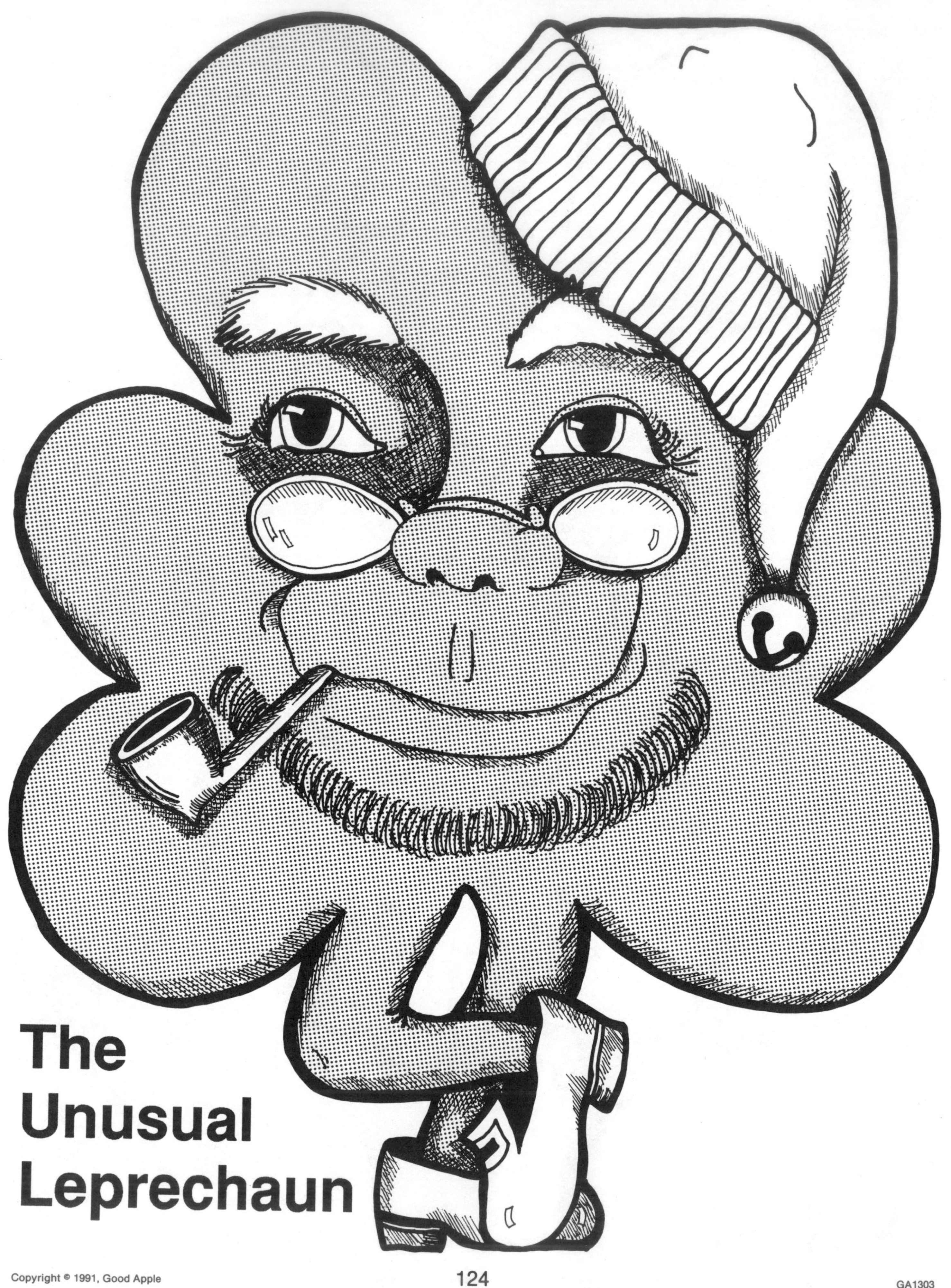

The Unusual Leprechaun

What YOU
Can Do for America

The Joyrider

The Castle Adventure

THE
DRINK

A GOOD SPORT
SPORTS FOR YOU

THE
BROKEN
WINDOW

THE
STRANGE
COMPUTER
ON
OFF

WILBUR'S
WOES

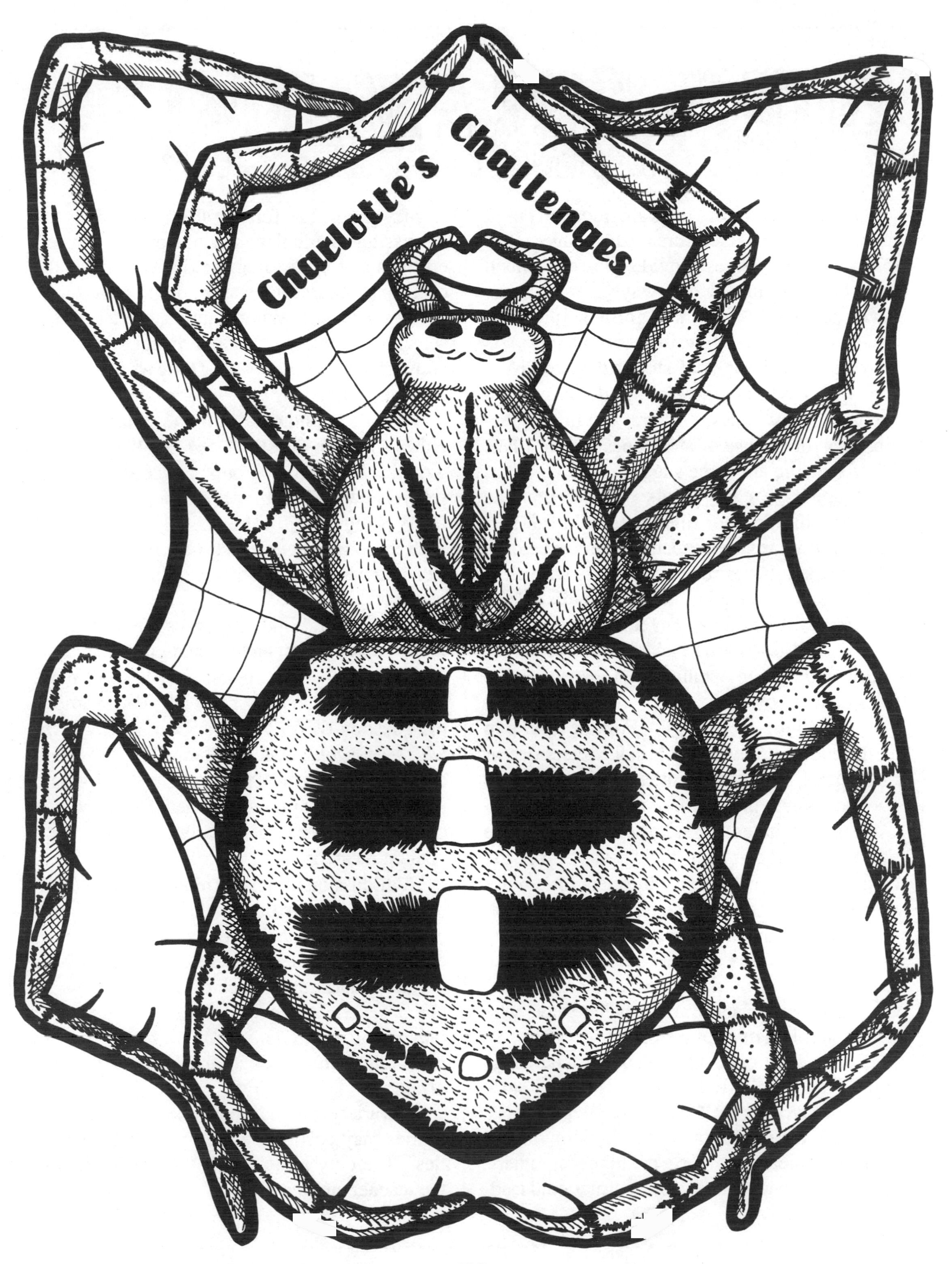
Charlotte's Challenges

QUESTIONS AND TITLES

Questions and story titles are frequently used to stimulate writers to create language. The following three pages provide questions which may be used in various ways for language development. A blank grid for new questions (to be prepared by writers or teachers) is provided. Five pages of story titles are given, followed by another blank grid for ease in preparing new ones. There are many possibilities for the use of story questions or titles. The following are some suggestions.

Preparation of Cards: Photocopy the pages of questions or titles onto colorful, stiff paper or onto regular paper and later glue onto heavy paper. If desired, cover pages with clear self-adhesive film. Cut into small cards. Place question cards inside an envelope for storage.

Place all title cards inside a box (or a container with a large opening) in a manner so the titles cannot be seen.

Classroom Activities: For the question cards students may either blindly select one or more cards, or they may intentionally select one question which they wish to answer in writing.

Have all students blindly select two or three title cards and return to their seats. From the cards drawn, each writer will select one to use as the title of a story which he or she will write.

Instead of the above preparation procedure, the pages of titles may be photocopied onto regular paper. Cut into either rows or columns. Give one **row** or **column** to each writer, who will then select **one** for a story.

For an activity developing the oral language skills, have each student ***tell*** a planned story instead of writing it. This procedure provides a precursor for writing activities by allowing all writers to hear the story creations of others. Through such an activity, the instructional leader may guide the future writing creations by discussing potential models of stories for selected titles and by leading the discussions of the oral contributions in an appropriate direction.

For a **group** writing activity, let a group select questions or titles in a manner described above. The members of the group *work together* to write a story.

Provide a photocopy of the blank grid of either titles or questions for small groups of writers. Have these groups collectively create several new questions or titles for future stories.

Writing Skills: The writing which occurs with these two types of stimuli may be at any step in the Five-Step Writing Plan explained on page 6.

The learners' first responses often appear at Step 1, and with much help and guidance in the writing process the responses will become more complete and carefully planned. For example, the question *Of all your personal possessions, which one would you most hate to lose?* might elicit an answer of *My bicycle* to a full length story about why one would hate to part with a computer because of how helpful and convenient it can be.

A discussion of writing models should occur early in these writing experiences. Sample models for questions and titles may be displayed on the chalkboard. An example of a model for the above question might be as follows: *Naming the possession one would hate to lose, one reason one would hate to lose it, other reasons one would hate to lose it, and a summary paragraph.*

A variety of additional exercises and activities may occur with these questions and titles. The only limitation is the imagination of the teacher and the writers.

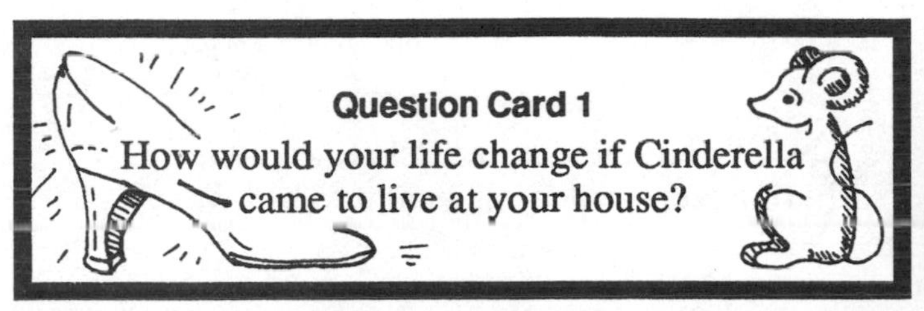

Question Card 1

How would your life change if Cinderella came to live at your house?

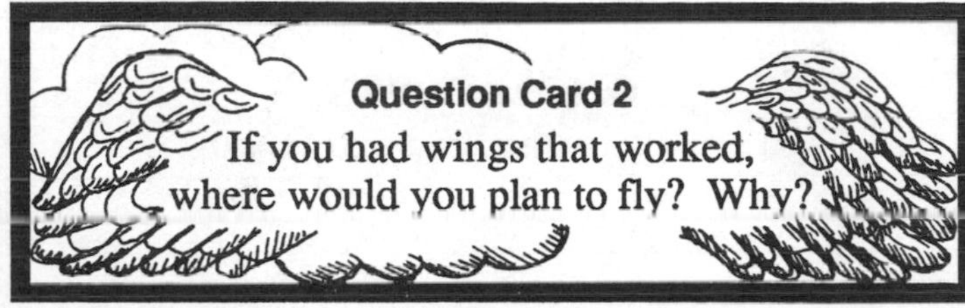

Question Card 2

If you had wings that worked, where would you plan to fly? Why?

Question Card 3

If you found a large sum of money, would you report it? Why or why not?

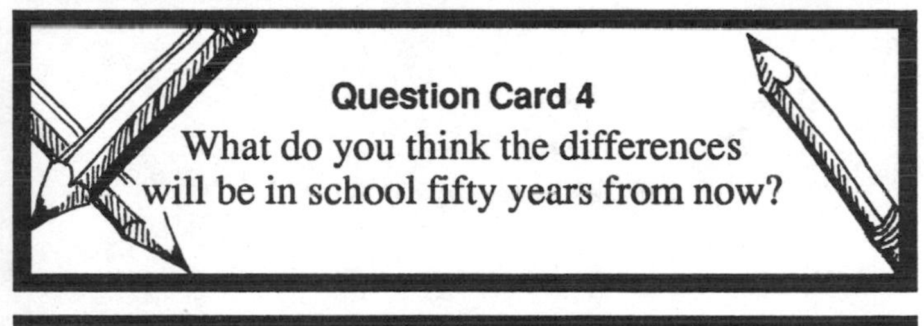

Question Card 4

What do you think the differences will be in school fifty years from now?

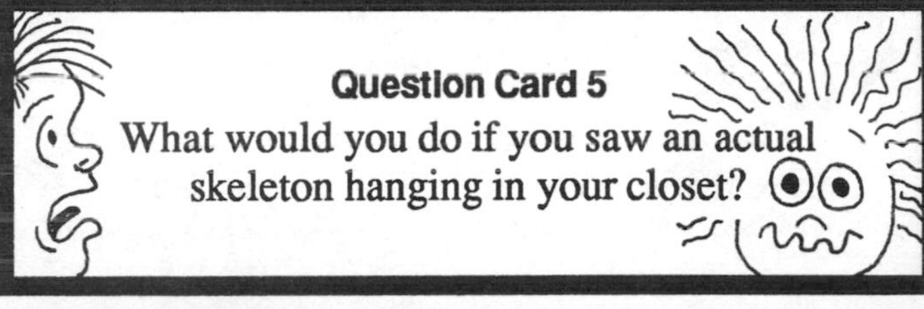

Question Card 5

What would you do if you saw an actual skeleton hanging in your closet?

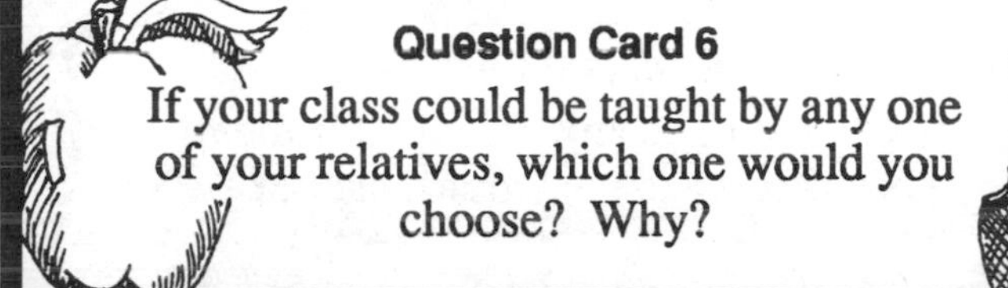

Question Card 6

If your class could be taught by any one of your relatives, which one would you choose? Why?

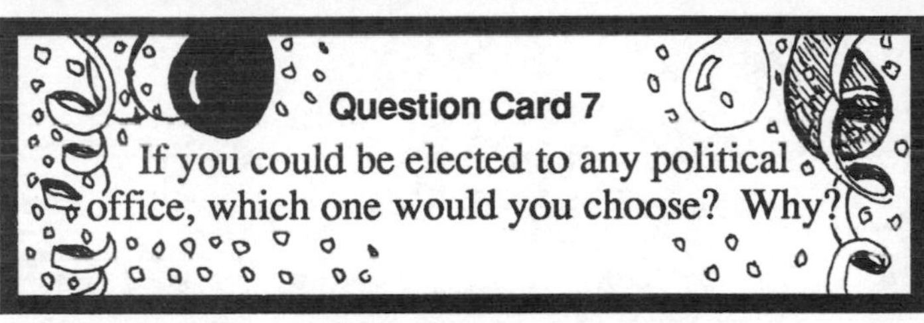

Question Card 7

If you could be elected to any political office, which one would you choose? Why?

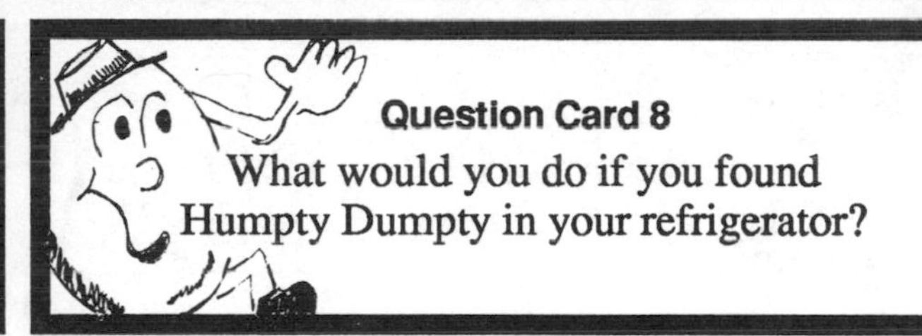

Question Card 8

What would you do if you found Humpty Dumpty in your refrigerator?

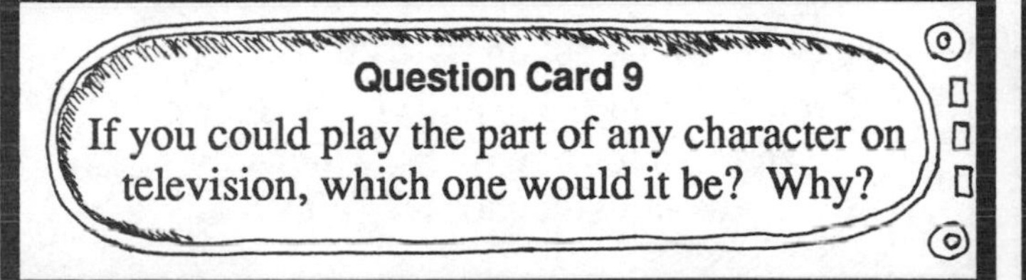

Question Card 9

If you could play the part of any character on television, which one would it be? Why?

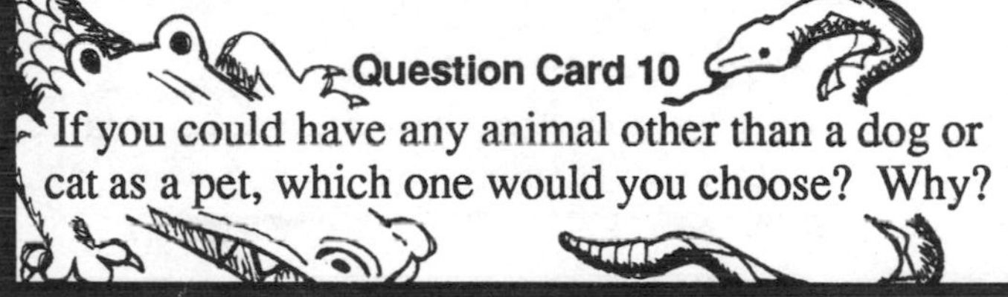

Question Card 10

If you could have any animal other than a dog or cat as a pet, which one would you choose? Why?

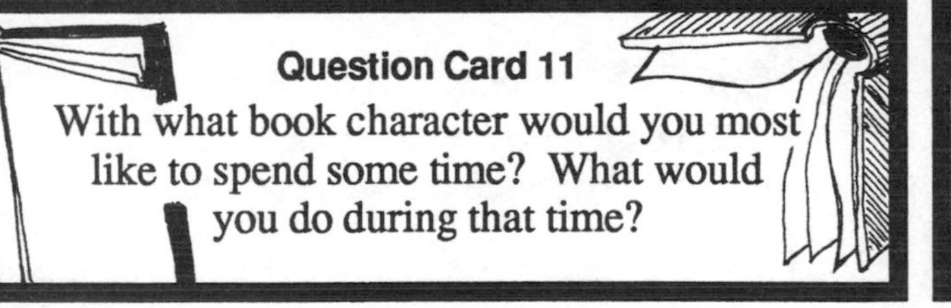

Question Card 11

With what book character would you most like to spend some time? What would you do during that time?

Question Card 12

What kind of conversation do you think the giant in "Jack and the Beanstalk" and the wolf in "The Three Little Pigs" might have?

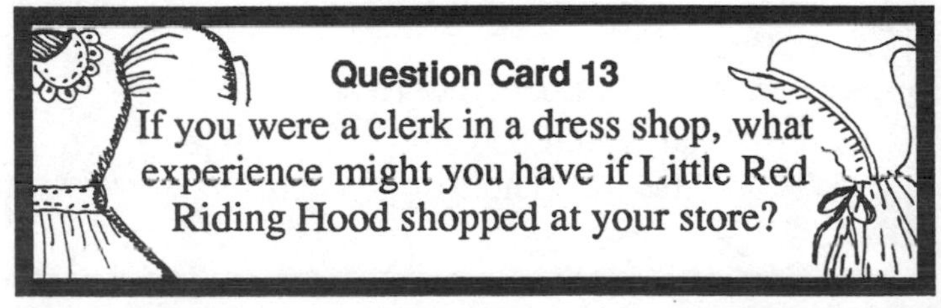

Question Card 13

If you were a clerk in a dress shop, what experience might you have if Little Red Riding Hood shopped at your store?

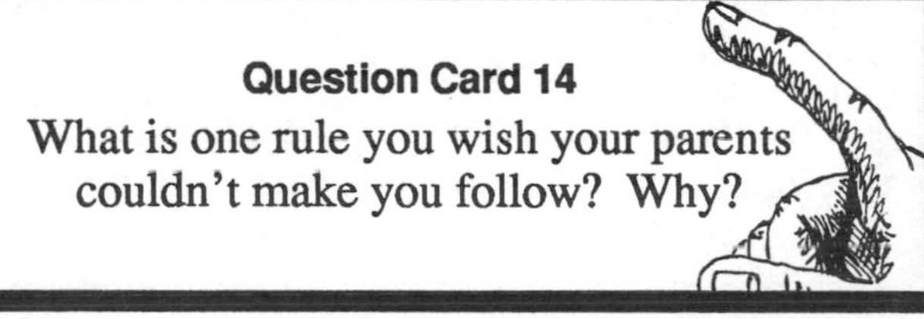

Question Card 14

What is one rule you wish your parents couldn't make you follow? Why?

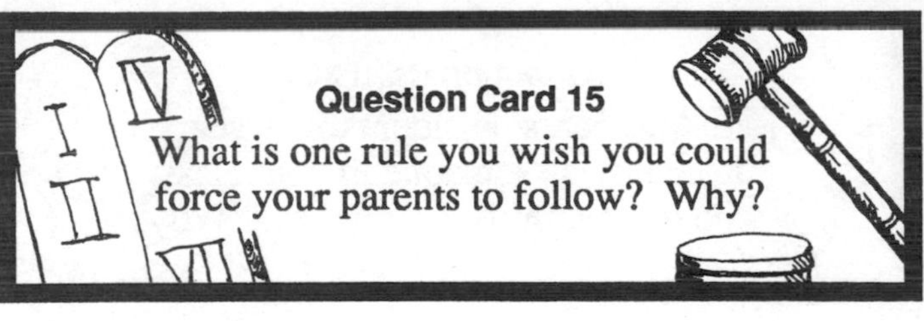

Question Card 15

What is one rule you wish you could force your parents to follow? Why?

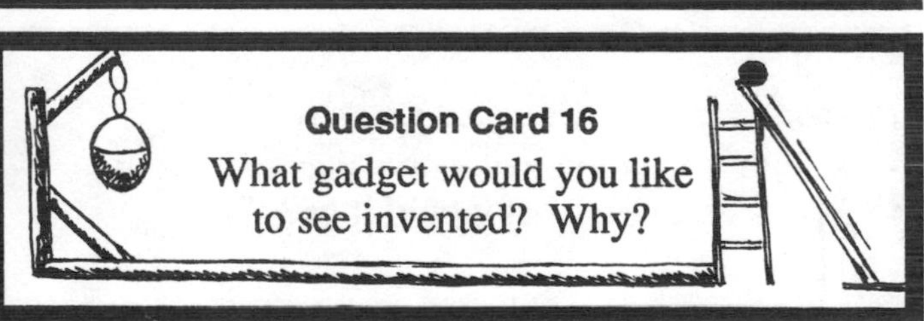

Question Card 16

What gadget would you like to see invented? Why?

Question Card 17

If your house had one extra room, what should it be used for? Why?

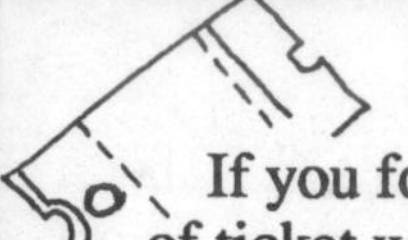

Question Card 18

If you found a free ticket, what kind of ticket would you want it to be? Why?

Question Card 19

If your school added a new subject, what would you want it to be? Why?

Question Card 20

If you found a baby elephant in your backyard, what would you do with it?

Question Card 21

If you could be any one **age** for the rest of your life, what age would that be? Why?

Question Card 22

What one thing could you do that would make the greatest number of people happy?

Question Card 23

If this were a school for witches, what do you think they would do during science class?

Question Card 24

How do you think you will describe your present year in school to your grandchildren?

Question Card 25

If you could have any **one** new feature on a car, what would you want? Why?

Question Card 26

If you could move to any city in the world and live for **one week,** which city would you choose? Why?

Question Card 27

What would be your plan to completely **fill the Grand Canyon?**

Question Card 28

If **birds** took over America, which bird would you like to see become president? Why?

Question Card 29

If you could add any one person as a new member to your family, who would it be? Why?

Question Card 30

What would be your plan to solve the world hunger problem?

Question Card 31

If you could make **one** change in your school, what would it be? Why?

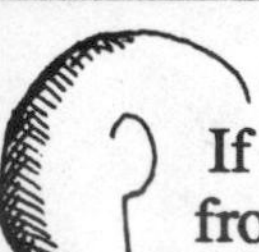

Question Card 32

If America's president thirty years from now is someone in your class, who do you think it would be? Why?

Question Card 33

If **your** favorite food became **everybody's** favorite food, how would this change most restaurants?

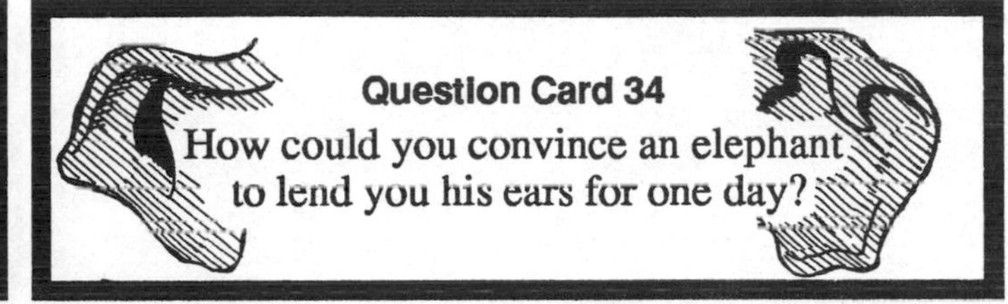

Question Card 34

How could you convince an elephant to lend you his ears for one day?

Question Card 35

If everything in the world turned one color, what color might it be? Why?

Question Card 36

If you could select any rock star or movie star to be the principal of your school, who would it be? Why?

Question Card 37

What present would you like to give everyone in your class? Why?

Question Card 38

What is the **worst** thing you have ever done to a friend? What kind of punishment do you deserve?

Question Card 39

What is the worst thing a friend has ever done to you? What kind of punishment should be given to that friend?

Question Card 40

If you had to drive one vehicle for the rest of your life, what kind of vehicle would it be? Why?

Question Card 41

What is the most frightened you have ever been? Why were you so scared?

Question Card 42

If you could be any sports hero for one day, who would you be? Why?

Question Card 43

If you were placed in a time machine and could dial any year of your life (past or present), what year would it be? What might that year be like?

Question Card 44

What do you think a dog's greatest wish in life might be? Why?

Question Card 45

If you had lived in the year 1700, what do you think your biggest problem might have been? Why?

Question Card 46

If a large egg had been left on your doorstep, what do you think it might hatch into? What would you do with it?

Question Card 47

If you saw your name on a "wanted" poster, what do you think your crime might have been?

Question Card 48

Of all of your personal possessions, which one would you most hate to lose? Why?

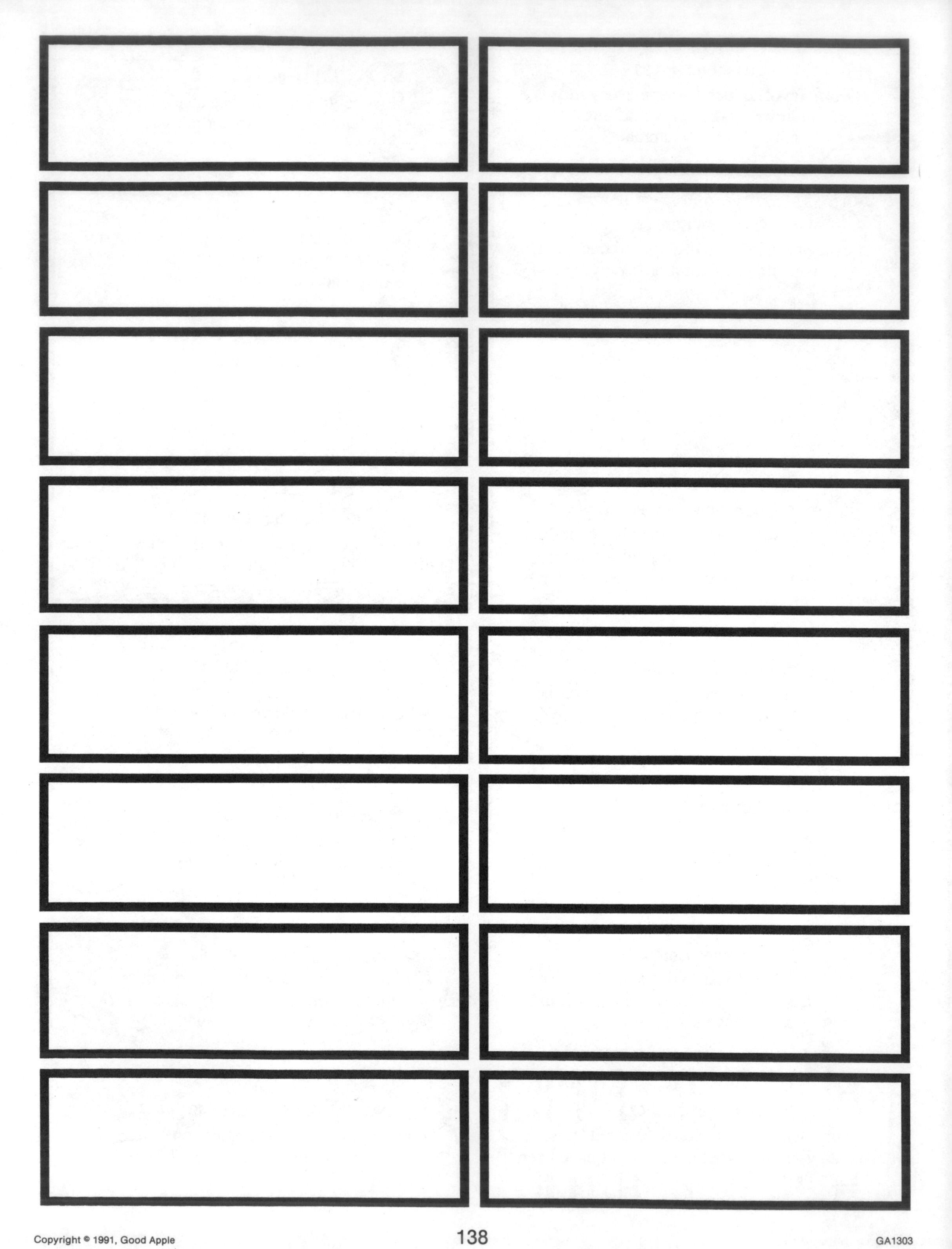

Transportation for the Year 3000

Creepy Footsteps

The Runaway Vacuum Cleaner

The Bashful Skunk

The Survivors!

A Day of School on Venus

The Missing Monster
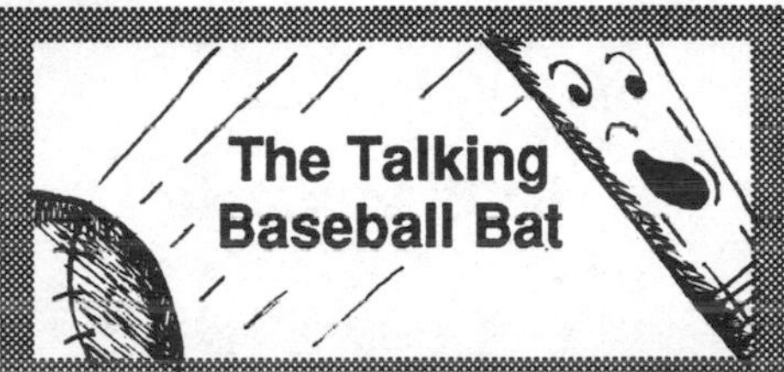
The Talking Baseball Bat

The Normal Nerd

The Gym Surprise

The Wandering Cyclops

The Nifty Gnomes

If I Had Thirty Sisters

The Peculiar Puppy

Five Fuzzy French Fries

The Rabid Robot

My Ten Pet Giraffes

Why Basketballs Were Invented

The Purple Dragon

Seventeen Snakes
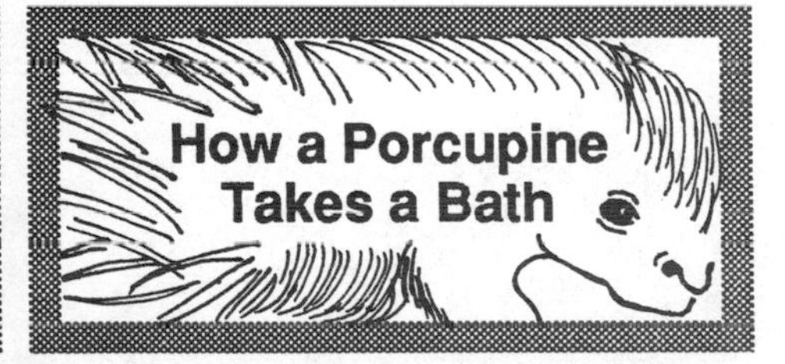
How a Porcupine Takes a Bath
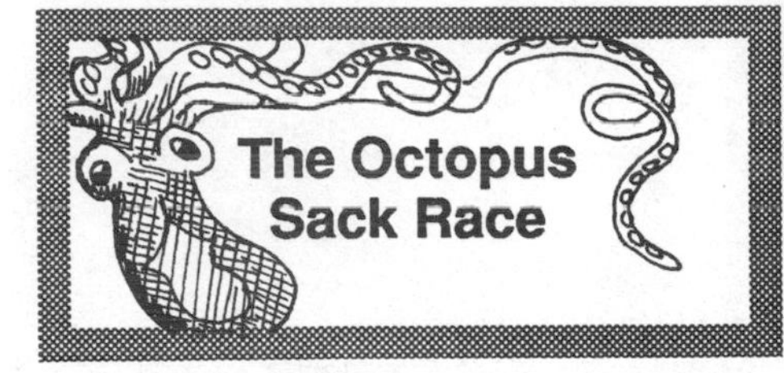
The Octopus Sack Race

How to Talk to a Cobra
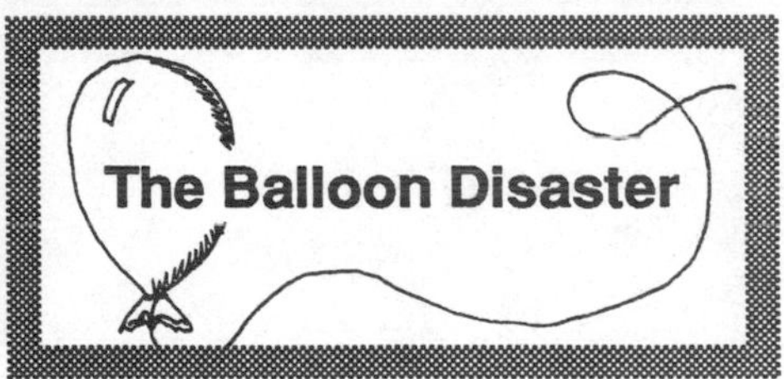
The Balloon Disaster

Next Year's Favorite Beverage

Making Shoes for a Centipede

The Freaked-Out Baseball

My Least Favorite Food

Nine Nervous Noises

The Midget's Magic

The Lost Luggage

The Extra Sock

The Turquoise Computer

Ten Tough Kids I Admire

The Poison Poem

The Baboon Cocoon

My Teacher's Biggest Headache

The Slam Dunker

The Political Poodle

The Strange Neighbor

The Scary Slumber Party

The Runaway Rock Star

A Fantastic Phone Call

The Disturbing Dream

The First Meal I Cooked

A Salary for My Cat

What I Will Tell My Grandchildren

A Contest I Hope to Win

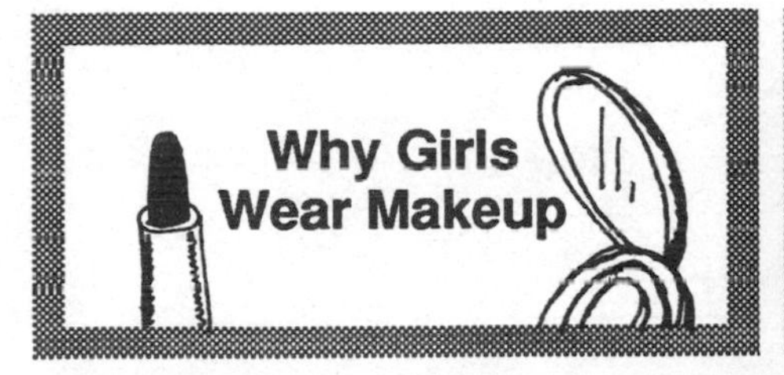
Why Girls
Wear Makeup

If Pens Had No Ink

The Elephant in
the Hot Air Balloon

My Greatest Fear

The Blast-Off

Fifty
Flying Saucers

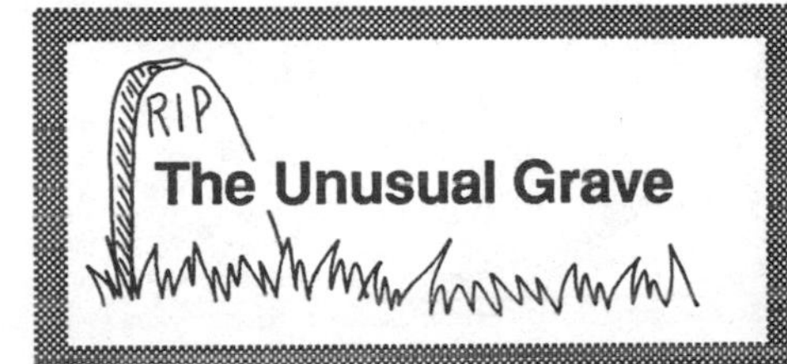
RIP
The Unusual Grave

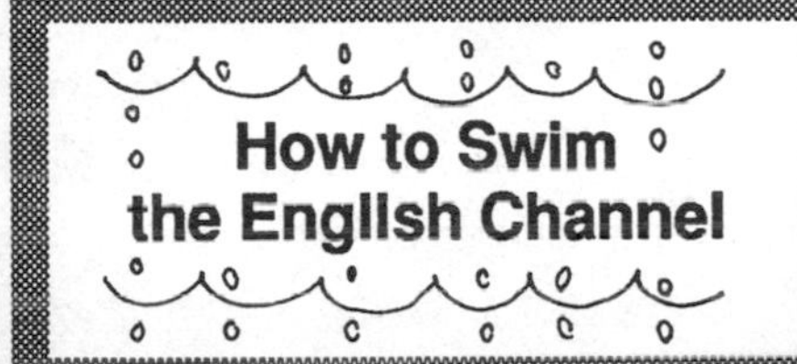
How to Swim
the English Channel

The Ostrich
That Wore Glasses

The Lovely Lizard

The Owl Who
Wore Contact Lenses

The Missing
Fireplace

Life Without
Buttons

Katie the Kite

The Day Things
Turned Green

Our Ninth Home

The Dark Door

Mouse Mischief

THUMP!

My Two-Faced
Neighbor

The Shy Santa

The Monkey with
No Manners

The Baby on
the Doorstep

The Peculiar Hat

My Date with Kelly

At the Barbershop

In the Middle of the Night

My Mom's Best Quality

Dad's Delight

No More Brothers!

The Car with Ten Tires

The Strange Fingerprint
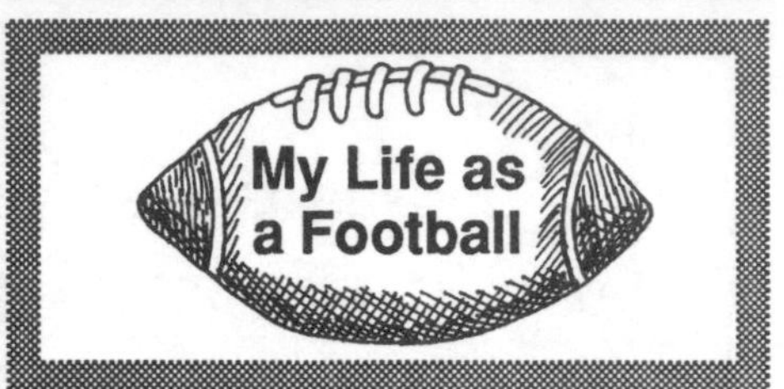
My Life as a Football

My Worst Fault
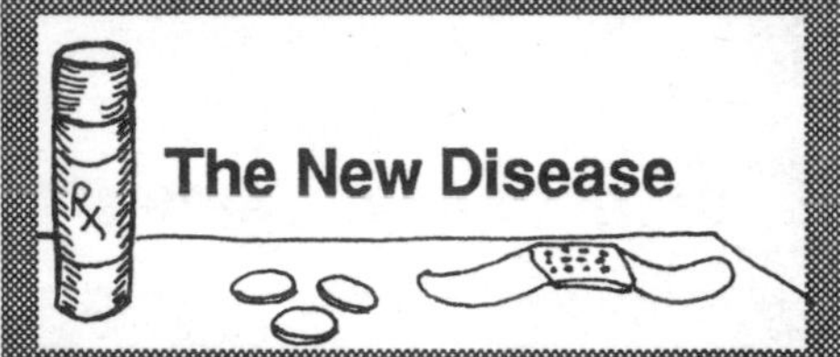
The New Disease

When I Become a Parent

The Day 2000 Pythons Escaped

My Lucky Number

The Three-Legged Spider
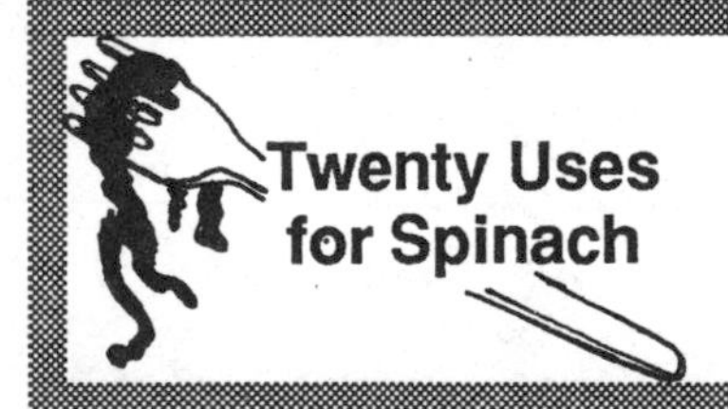
Twenty Uses for Spinach

Music in the Year 2050

The Donkey's Dilemma

The Gorgeous Ghost

The Living T-Shirt

Love at First Fright

Two New School Rules
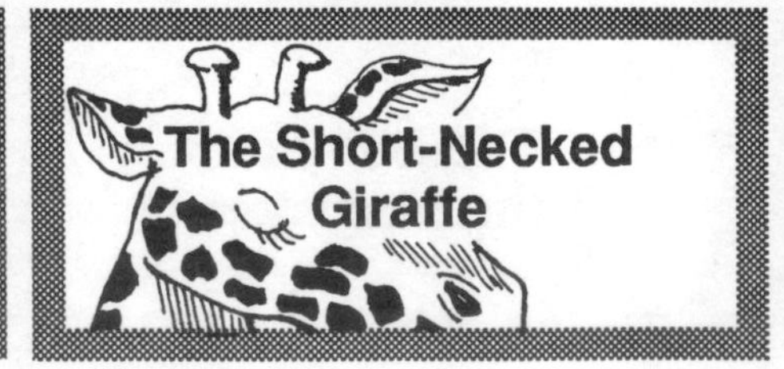
The Short-Necked Giraffe

The Camel with Four Humps

My Friend's
Wedding

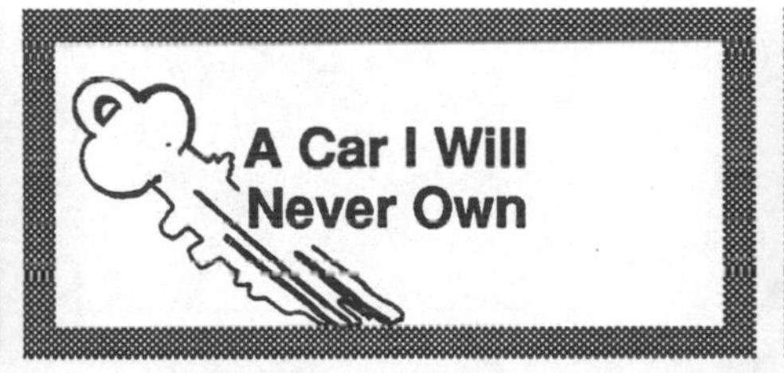
A Car I Will
Never Own

My Choice
for President

Why I'm Great!

The Two Wishes

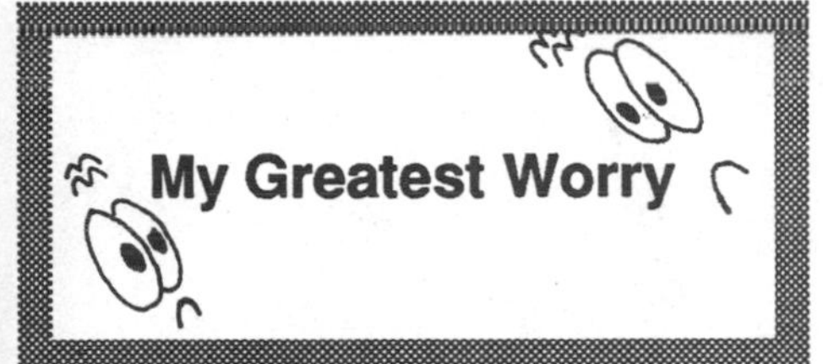
My Greatest Worry

My View of Fun

Lucy's Black Eye

The Magic Book

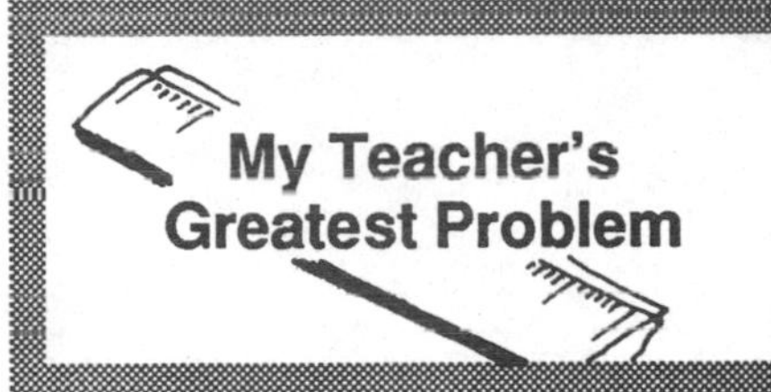
My Teacher's
Greatest Problem

The Talkative
Tiger

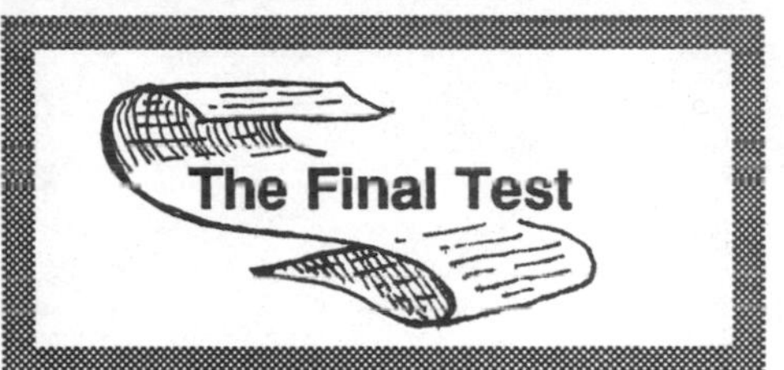
The Final Test

The Fatal Fire

The Ghost's
Problem

My Dog Thinks
He Is a Person

The Future
of Homework

The Purpose
of War

The Orange Hippo

My Former Friend

The Brilliant Bear

In the Attic

If Abraham Lincoln
Were Alive

The Pigs'
Pajama Party

My New Invention

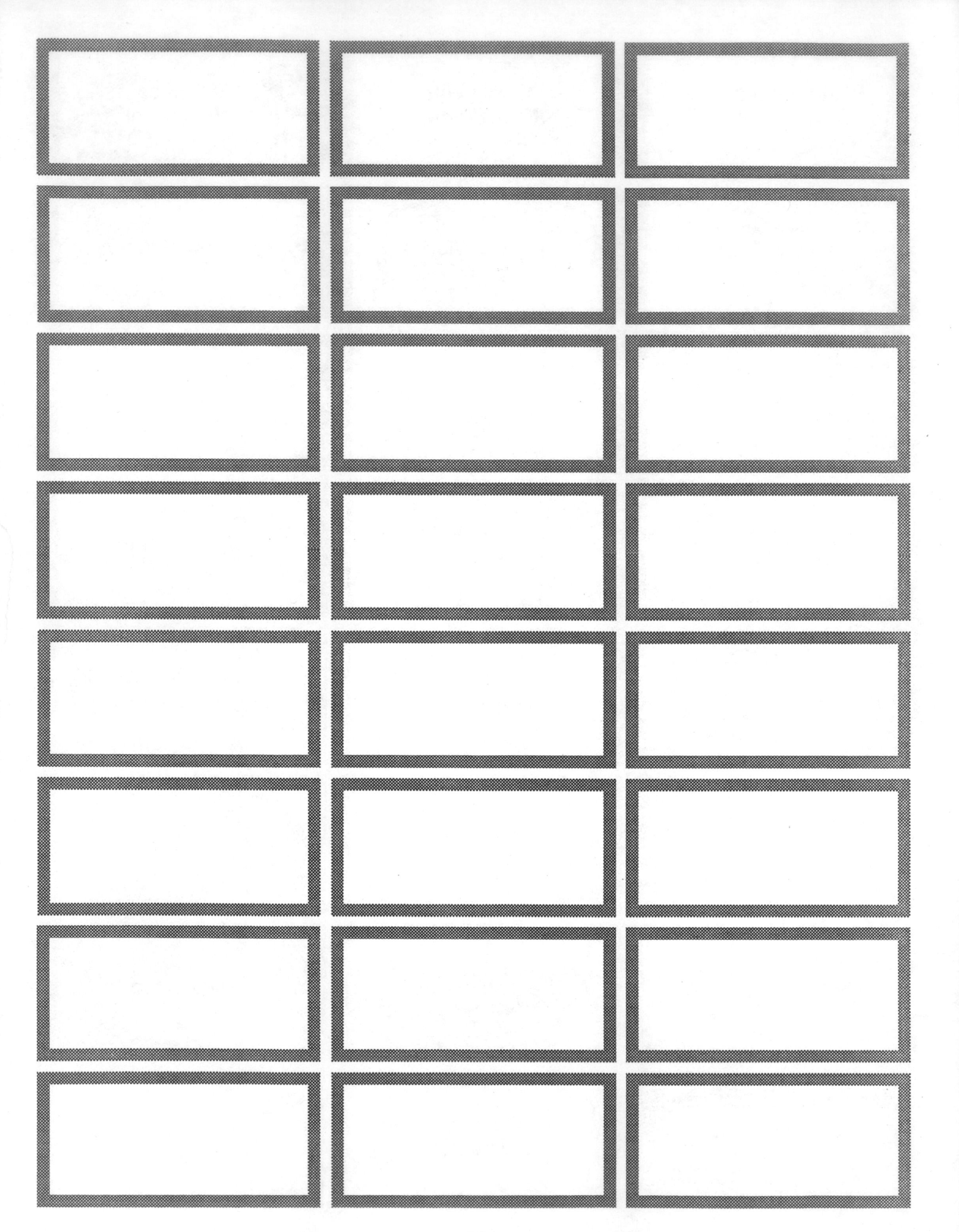